UNNAMED

UNNAMED

Unsuspecting HEROES
Singled Out by God

CHRIS TRAVIS

Standard®
PUBLISHING

Cincinnati, Ohio

Published by Standard Publishing, Cincinnati, Ohio

www.standardpub.com

Copyright © 2010 by Standard Publishing

Also available: *Unnamed Group Member Discussion Guide,* ISBN 978-0-7847-7440-3, copyright © 2010 by Standard Publishing

Printed in: United States of America

Project editor: Lynn Lusby Pratt

Cover design: Claudine Mansour

Interior design: Dina Sorn at Ahaa! Design

ISBN 978-0-7847-7439-7

Library of Congress Cataloging-in-Publication Data

Travis, Chris, 1977-
   Unnamed : unsuspecting heroes singled out by God / Chris Travis.
      p. cm.
   Includes bibliographical references and index.
   ISBN 978-0-7847-7439-7 (perfect bound : alk. paper)
   1. Heroes in the Bible--Biography. 2. Bible--Biography. I. Title.
BS579.H4T73 2010
220.9'2--dc22
                                             2009038365

15 14 13 12 11 10   1 2 3 4 5 6 7 8 9

DEDICATION

TO MY WIFE, LINDSAY.
Of all of God's unsung heroes,
she's my favorite.

ACKNOWLEDGMENTS

Given the title and message of this book, it's ironic that mine is the only name on the cover. So many others shared in its creation. I love that I get to name some of them here:

Lindsay Black, thank you for thinking of me for this book.

Dale Reeves, thank you for making it seem like I'm a better writer than I am.

Lynn Pratt, thank you for the idea of asking people for untold stories about everyday heroes—and for catching every little thing.

Larry Bennett, thank you for asking how the writing was going almost every time we spoke.

Lawrence and Patricia Travis, thank you for all the edits and suggestions, and for still being my mom and dad, even into my adulthood.

Lindsay Travis, thank you for reading everything while it was still very rough, and for encouraging me anyways. Thank you for being my partner in this book, as you have been in all things.

To everyone who contributed stories of unnamed heroes: Thank you for writing so much of this book for me.

To God's Unnamed Heroes: Thank you for looking after orphans and widows in their distress; for courageously following God through fire, war, and famine; for logging countless hours at 9-to-5s, financing God's work in the world; for your beautiful creativity; for believing in God in the midst of pain; for praying; for loving the lost, the broken, and your enemies; and for all the other ways you've inspired the writing of this book.

CONTENTS

UNNAMED

God works primarily through everyday people.

This is the only life that you are ever going to get on this earth.

How's it going? Like you expected?

Have you accomplished what you hoped you would, or are you still hacking away at it?

Or have you decided to throw in the towel and give up altogether?

Perhaps you were told that you could "be anything you want to be" when you grew up. If you just believed in yourself and worked really hard, you could be an astronaut, a rock star, or even the president of the United States.

I'm not so sure that's true. I think there are variables involved beyond just confidence and hard work. I'm also not so sure it matters. There are deeper things. Truer things. There are things that are more important than your circumstances. There are things that will last a whole lot longer. We make decisions with outcomes that matter so much more than any achievements, awards, job titles, or accomplishments. We can make a difference that will last so much longer than any name we could make for ourselves in this world.

Most of the "greatest people who ever lived" have been forgotten. Don't believe me? How many people can you name who lived three thousand years ago? For the truly great people, it may take one hundred years for their memory to be erased. Some epic heroes stake out a name that people remember for a thousand years. The vast majority of people, no matter how great, simply vanish from the earth. James, one of Jesus' brothers, observed, "What is your life? You are a mist that appears for a little while and then vanishes" (James 4:14, *NIV*).

Most of the "greatest people who ever lived" have been forgotten.

Yet we all long for something more. God "has planted eternity in the human heart" (Ecclesiastes 3:11). We want our lives to matter—we want to know that we've made a difference. We want our efforts to count for something. We want to be a part of something that is bigger than we are, and that lasts longer than this life does. "But even so," as the rest of that verse explains, "people cannot see the whole scope of God's work from beginning to end."

EVERYDAY PEOPLE

I find it fascinating that some of the heroes in the Bible are unnamed. God included in the Bible the accounts of dozens of these people. Though they contributed to God's story, their names—as often happens in everyday, modern life—are not recorded.

Some did very small things. Others performed outlandish heroics. An unnamed princess rescued baby Moses from the river. An unnamed young man saved Paul's life. Unnamed heroes participated in miracles, celebrated victory over entire armies, and surprised God himself with their faith.

The Bible says, "Each one should use whatever gift he has received to serve others, faithfully administering God's grace in its various forms" (1 Peter 4:10, *NIV*). *Each one* of us. Not just some of us; not only the great among us; not only those who are paid to serve in the church; not only those of us who make a name for ourselves—each one of us is gifted by God. Each one of us should use our gifts to administer the various forms of God's grace. Sometimes God works miracles. Occasionally, he sends an angel. Normally, though, he administers his grace through everyday people.

God certainly orchestrates circumstances. If the Bible were a symphony, from time to time we'd hear the cymbal clash of his mighty works, but it wouldn't be the melody line. Over the ominous rumbling of timpani drums and the pounding bass signifying evil and death would rise the violins, the horns, the trilling flutes telling tales of the lives of people, played by the hands of God. He himself became an everyday person—a carpenter's son, born to a young mother, raised in a no-place town.

Sometimes God works miracles. Occasionally, he sends an angel. Normally, though, he administers his grace through everyday people.

Read the Bible from cover to cover, and you will find that God works primarily through everyday people—at least, that is the part of his work he focused on recording for us. The Bible is the story of how God met, prompted, and empowered people to live out his will and achieve his purposes. The Bible is the story of God using everyday people—people just like you. The story isn't about us; it's about God. And he's much more than simply the main character. He's "the author and perfecter of our faith" (Hebrews 12:2, *NIV*).

What he does with everyday people is more beautiful than any poem, aria, or epic. God's work to turn everyday people into heroes is the crowning glory of his creation. "For we are God's masterpiece. He has created us anew in Christ Jesus, so we can do the good things he planned for us long ago" (Ephesians 2:10).

EVERYDAY HEROES

Long ago, God planned good things for us to do. Good things that would impact people. Ask anyone about his or her most important moment in life or journey toward faith, and you will find, almost always, the influence of everyday people woven into the tale.

But you have to *ask*. Most of the work of God's heroes goes unnoticed and unrecorded. Sometimes their stories make the news; more often they do not. Most of the work of God's heroes is significant, important, and even history-changing. But it is seldom flashy. It's usually not glamorous enough for this world to take notice.

> Most of the work of God's heroes is significant, important, and even history-changing. But it is seldom flashy.

As I prepared to write this book, I asked. I sent out messages to my network of people and asked them to share with me untold stories of God's heroes. I asked them to share with me stories they knew of people making sacrifices, taking risks, or heroically doing the right thing—preferably stories that hadn't made the news. I hoped that I would hear about ways they'd seen everyday heroes working in the background. I was sure that God was up to a whole lot more in people's lives than we normally get a look at.

I had no idea.

The overwhelming response I received was one of the most faith-affirming experiences of my life. God's unnamed heroes are literally changing the world—just as tiny lights can transform an entire room of darkness; just as a few grains of salt can flavor an entire meal. I can't wait to share some of these stories with you. If you have any doubt about the activity of God expressed through people today, read on. If the negative press about the church has gotten under your skin or chipped away at your faith, read on.

YOUR HEROIC POTENTIAL

Long ago, God planned good things for *you* to do. Your life may never be flashy. You may never be recognized. If I were laying bets, my money would be on the world forgetting all about you and me both not long after we've passed on. But there are things that last forever. There are rewards that are so much better than recognition and fame. Unnamed people can have a more significant impact on the world than the president of the United States, than rock stars, than astronauts.

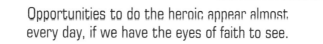

Opportunities to do the heroic appear almost every day, if we have the eyes of faith to see.

In this book, we'll take a look at eight of the Bible's unnamed heroes. Each chapter will introduce an unnamed man, woman, or child who became one of God's unlikely heroes. The stories of these unnamed heroes give us insight into how God wants to fill our lives with adventure, significance, and lasting impact. Each chapter concludes with some questions to help reveal your own heroic potential, and specific action steps you can take to "do the good things he planned for us long ago."

I believe that if you'll take the time to read through and consider what these stories mean for us today, you will begin to see how God intends to use your life to accomplish his purposes. Opportunities to do the heroic appear almost every day, if we have the eyes of faith to see. And all those reasons that you think could disqualify you from being powerfully used by God will melt away. You'll find the courage to act.

At this point, don't worry if you doubt. Don't worry if you fear. Don't worry if it all sounds a little unlikely and grandiose. Those feelings are all part of it really. I wasn't kidding when I said that God works primarily through *everyday* people.

The Bible is the lens through which we see reality. I'm only asking you to look through the lens. Through the lens of these eight Bible passages, look at God, at the world, at life—at your own life—and see what comes into focus.

ONE

UNEXPECTED

2 KINGS 5:1-14

God prompts unexpected heroes to do the unexpected.

Sometimes my life just feels like the same old thing.

5:50 AM. *Beep! Beep! Beep!* Smack the snooze button.

5:59 AM. *Beep! Beep! Beep!* Groan. Shower. Shave. Button. Tie. Coffee. Commute. Same work as yesterday. Commute. Family. Chores. TV. Set alarm. Sleep.

5:50 AM. *Beep! Beep! Beep!* Groan . . .

Of course, things happen . . . sometimes. Sometimes there's a victory at work. Sometimes there's a special occasion with my family or friends. Sometimes something truly unexpected happens. But most days run together into a blur of responsibilities and duties. Most days I do not expect to do anything more significant than I did the previous day.

I'm sure the details of your life are different from mine. Maybe your

days cycle around classes and studying or taking care of your kids or land-
ing the next contract. But while the details are different, you'd probably
agree that we can all get into a rut. Something pulls us—drags us—toward
the mundane. The cynic in us smirks at the notion that daily life could be
exciting. It can start to feel as if it's not worth the effort to make something
extraordinary happen.

Seriously, how many mornings do you down a glass of orange juice and
bound out the door, ready to change the world? When was the last time
you faced your day as a hero would—ready to save the innocent, defeat
the enemy, or champion a just cause? Be honest. Do you really expect the
unexpected?

Then why do we long for it?

> ## It can start to feel as if it's not worth the effort
> ## to make something extraordinary happen.

I don't want a work-family-church-vacation-work-repeat kind of life. At
least, that's not *all* that I want. I want to change things. I want to have an impact. And I want my life—my everyday life, not just those really rare days—
to be filled with adventure. I want to be surprised from time to time. I'd even
like to surprise myself occasionally. I think saying the words "I didn't know I
had it in me!" might feel even better than a pay raise.

And I don't think I'm alone. In fact, I'd bet that in spite of whatever
differences there are between us, you and I have at least this one thing in
common: we both want our lives to matter. If life could be interesting,
even better, Is it too much to ask for it to be thrilling? There must be more
to life than the mere routine of staying alive. It's not that the routines are
unimportant, but there must be *more*.

I'd like to suggest that there are reasons why we long for the unexpected and yet still see the same day after day. Our own expectations have become a blindfold to the deeper realities. We expect today to be like every other day. Those expectations can disguise all the extraordinary opportunities for us to do the unexpected. And it is in doing the unexpected that you often find heroism.

What if we're looking at things the wrong way? Colossians 4:5 tells us to "make the most of every opportunity." But we could be missing opportunities to do the heroic because we don't even know how to recognize them.

There is a story in the Bible about an everyday person who did something unexpected, and it changed everything. And there's a message in this story for us today about the hidden narrative of life—the bigger, truer story that's unfolding amid our daily grind. If we grasp the implications of this message, it will help us begin to see our daily lives as they really are: filled with incredible moments for adventure. If we can learn how to see the true story of life, we'll find that our days call for courage and a willingness to do the unexpected.

WHEN THE UNEXPECTED HAPPENS

The hero in our story would be easy to overlook, because by any earthly standard she seems so insignificant. She appears only in a few short verses at the beginning of 2 Kings 5. Only one verse of Scripture records anything about what she actually did. We don't know much about her at all.

We don't even know her name.

But because this girl recognized the potential of a seemingly ordinary moment, she did something unexpected—and changed the possibilities for an entire nation.

Sound a little grandiose? That's your cynical side talking.

All we know about where she came from is that "Aramean raiders had invaded the land of Israel, and among their captives was a young girl"

(2 Kings 5:2). Raiders captured her. That brief biography says a lot. Maybe she awoke to an eerie calm, sensing something in the darkness. She strained to hear. Her eyes widened when she felt it—a tremor in the earth. Then she heard the distant rumble and tried to will it away. But now it was unmistakable—the thunder of hoof on turf—the dreadful herald of two terrifying words: Aramean raiders.

The nation of Israel had been through multiple campaigns of war against the Arameans (also called Syrians). The two nations had assaulted one another ruthlessly. When God pronounced his judgments on the nations through the prophet Amos, he denounced the Arameans of Damascus for wartime cruelty: "They beat down my people in Gilead as grain is threshed with iron sledges" (Amos 1:3).

Imagine the screams as the slave girl's neighbors and family awoke to this real-life nightmare of torches, bared teeth, and snorting horses. Raiders ripped open the tents and ransacked the dwellings. Swords flashed. Horses, wide-eyed and flecked with foam, reared and stamped the air. Perhaps men kicked this unnamed girl to the ground, then dragged her by her hair. Maybe they tied her, hand and foot, and slung her over a saddle, or tethered her to the horn and forced her to run. Later, she would shudder whenever she wondered what happened to the people who had not been taken.

Maybe we don't want the unexpected to happen as much as we think we do.

Imagine the screams as the slave girl's neighbors and family awoke to this real-life nightmare of torches, bared teeth, and snorting horses.

We don't know the precise details of her capture, but we know where she ended up. She "had been given to Naaman's wife as a maid" (2 Kings 5:2). She was a slave in the household of Naaman. Of all the people in Aram—

Naaman! He was the head commander of the Aramean armies. He was the one ultimately in charge of the terrifying raiders. This Israelite girl served the man who was *responsible* for her captivity. She washed his things, took care of his wife, and obeyed his daily commands.

Unlike our hero, Naaman certainly had a name for himself. He was greatly admired by the Aramean king as a valiant warrior who led Aram in many victories over Israel. But with all Naaman had going for him, he had one problem—one critical weakness that outweighed all of it: "Though Naaman was a mighty warrior, he suffered from leprosy" (v. 1).

Leprosy was perhaps the most feared, shunned, and alienating disease in biblical times. Some forms of skin infection were so nasty and contagious that people in that day didn't bother to distinguish between them. If you had a skin disease of any kind, you were considered a leper, and the message from the people was clear: stay away. Naaman apparently had sections of skin that were as "white as snow" (see v. 27). How weary he must have been of people trying not to stare. Even with armies of fearsome warriors at his disposal, how powerless he must have felt.

From the perspective of a slave girl ripped from her home, this dread disease might be exactly what we would expect: a little justice. This powerful man whose command brought misery to innocent people was being punished for it. *Serves him right*, you might think. A captive in Naaman's house could get a lot of satisfaction from his suffering.

HEROES DO THE UNEXPECTED

Of course, maybe the slave girl's capture hadn't been quite so violent. Maybe she hadn't left any family behind. Maybe she was an orphan. Maybe she had surrendered and been treated civilly by the invaders. We don't know. But we can at least say that she had been carried into a foreign land where her faith was abhorred. They had taken her from her home and taken her freedom. Most people would be writhing with bitterness toward this commander who was responsible for it. Each day of tidying up after him and fetching things for his wife would have ground bitter salt into the wound.

But this unnamed girl did the unexpected. Second Kings 5:3 says, "One day the girl said to her mistress, 'I wish my master would go to see the prophet in Samaria. He would heal him of his leprosy.'" She looked at Naaman's plight with compassion. She offered a solution—told about where he could get help. She showed him kindness. Had she forgiven him for the situation he'd put her in?

What a moment. What a glimpse into God's unexpected plan! Just as through a tiny keyhole we can see the vast outdoors, through the servant girl's tiny kindness we can see the blessed irony of grace.

This powerless slave girl had the answer to her captor's greatest need. She didn't do what we might have expected. But then again, "God chose things the world considers foolish in order to shame those who think they are wise. And he chose things that are powerless to shame those who are powerful" (1 Corinthians 1:27). We'd expect justice, but God gives grace. And as we discover here, so do his heroes.

What courage this girl had! What must it have taken for her to speak up? She had everything to lose and nothing to gain. Captured by raiders and taken from her homeland and from the worship of the Lord, she certainly had ample reason to doubt God's power. Perhaps God was no longer even with her. Why, Naaman might take her seriously and actually travel all the way to Israel in hopes of an impossible healing. The girl seemed to have true faith in God's prophet, but what if something went wrong?

There are so many other things she might have said (if we would expect her to have said anything at all). We might have expected her to put a price on this valuable information. She held the key to unlock a powerful man from his prison of discomfort and stigma, yet she didn't ask for a single penny. We would have expected her to at least ask for her freedom. In an unexpected reversal of fortune, she was holding all the cards, yet she didn't even ask to travel back to Israel along with Naaman.

This unnamed hero did what we might least expect. Instead of demanding justice, she offered grace. Instead of shrinking back, she spoke up in faith. And instead of acting on her own behalf, she focused on meeting the needs of her enemy.

A man named Julio Diaz did something similar in February 2008.[1]

The thirty-one-year-old social worker had gotten off his subway commute home to the Bronx—as he did every night—to eat at his favorite diner. As he walked toward the stairs on the nearly empty platform, his evening took an unexpected turn. A teenage boy pulled a knife on him.

She held the key to unlock a powerful man from his prison of discomfort and stigma, yet she didn't ask for a single penny.

Diaz handed over his wallet. But as the boy turned away, Diaz called after him, "Hey, wait a minute. You forgot something. If you're going to be robbing people for the rest of the night, you might as well take my coat to keep you warm."

The boy's shock gave Diaz the chance to say more: "If you're willing to risk your freedom for a few dollars, then I guess you must really need the money. I mean, all I wanted to do was get dinner and if you really want to join me . . . hey, you're more than welcome."

The stunned teenager agreed. While they were eating, people kept coming over to greet Diaz   the manager, the waiters, even the dishwashers. The boy wondered if Diaz owned the place, but Diaz explained that he was just a regular.

"But you're even nice to the dishwasher," the teen said.

"Well, haven't you been taught you should be nice to everybody?" Diaz replied.

"Yeah, but I didn't think people actually behaved that way."

When the bill arrived, there was an awkward moment. Diaz said, "If you give me my wallet back, I'll gladly treat you." The teenager did, and Diaz not only paid for dinner but also gave his would-be robber a $20 bill. But he did ask for something in return—the knife.

Then the boy did something we never would have expected from the same guy who had first approached Diaz on that platform. He took out the knife and handed it over.

UNEXPECTED RESULTS

The slave girl's simple suggestion sparked a chain reaction of unexpected events. Naaman sought permission from his king to travel to Israel to find the prophet who supposedly could heal him. The king of Aram agreed, and at once drafted a letter to the king of Israel. Because if somebody in Israel could heal like that, you'd expect that he would answer to the king.

Naaman departed for Israel, leading a train of chariots and horses loaded down with hundreds of pounds of gold and silver to offer in exchange for this unbelievable miracle. Because if somebody in Israel could heal like that, you'd expect it to cost a fortune.

But when the king of Israel read the letter from the king of Aram, asking that he heal Naaman of leprosy, he panicked. He tore his robes and cried out: "This man sends me a leper to heal! Am I God, that I can give life and take it away? I can see that he's just trying to pick a fight with me" (2 Kings 5:7).

Elisha, the powerful man of God, heard about the king of Israel tearing his robes, and sent a message to the king: "Why are you so upset? Send Naaman to me, and he will learn that there is a true prophet here in Israel" (v. 8).

So as the unnamed slave girl worked at her chores back in Aram, Naaman appeared before Elisha's house with his entourage of horses and chariots, expecting an audience with the great prophet. He was following the courtly etiquette that governed how important people approached one another. But Elisha didn't even come out. Naaman, the great commander, waited at the door, perhaps in fine array of glittering armor, bearing hundreds of pounds of gold and silver, and Elisha didn't even come out. Instead, he sent a messenger with a very simple prescription: "Go and wash yourself seven times in the Jordan River. Then your skin will be restored, and you will be healed of your leprosy" (v. 10).

This infuriated Naaman. "'I thought he would certainly come out to meet me!' he said. 'I expected him to wave his hand over the leprosy and call on the name of the LORD his God and heal me!'" (v. 11). It was too much for Naaman's pride. He had come all this way on the advice of a slave girl. He had left the courts of the king to visit this alleged prophet, who didn't even bother to come out to meet him. Didn't this Elisha know who he was?

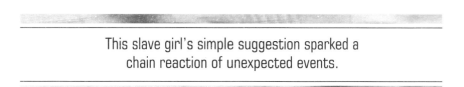

This slave girl's simple suggestion sparked a chain reaction of unexpected events.

And "go and wash yourself seven times in the Jordan River"? The Jordan? Weren't the rivers in Damascus better than all the rivers in Israel combined? Was he being mocked? Naaman was enraged, and he stormed off.

His officers tried to reason with him. "Sir, if the prophet had told you to do something very difficult, wouldn't you have done it? So you should certainly obey him when he says simply, 'Go and wash and be cured!'" (v. 13). They managed to persuade him. The text says that Naaman went down to the Jordan River and dipped himself seven times in the water.

Picture this: The chariots, the horses, the warriors, the gleaming weapons and armor—the splendor of the great commander's mighty escort—impressively lined up along the banks of the river. Naaman dismounts. He looks at the river and . . . sighs? shrugs? rolls his eyes? Attendants come and begin to unbuckle the panels of his armor. One takes his sword. Naaman disrobes and stands before his entourage in his undergarments. Then he makes his way down the bank and wades into the river. Maybe he grimaced at the silt that stirred up around his waist.

I like to imagine his internal dialogue. What must he have been thinking after each dip into the river?

He goes under once. *This is ridiculous . . . a waste of time . . . I should never have come on this journey . . .*

He dips again. *But I do hope this works . . .*

A third time. *If this doesn't work, then there's nothing else for me to do.*

He dips a fourth time. *I bet my men are laughing at me.*

A fifth time. *I bet she's laughing at me . . . that slave girl.*

He dips a sixth time. *I should stop. Nothing's happening. If I back out now, I could at least hold on to some dignity. I could say I knew all along that this was a hoax. I could say that I went along with it to incite our people to war. I could . . . oh, but it has to work. It has to! Oh God, I can't live like this. All the strength you've given me, my command, my power—it means nothing to me if I'm just going to rot on my feet. Please save me!*

He holds his breath. He hopes. He goes under the seventh time. "And his skin became as healthy as . . . a young child's, and he was healed!" (v. 14).

Imagine how he must have reacted! Imagine him staring at his perfect skin in disbelief as this new reality made its way to his heart. And then he forgot himself. He shouted! He splashed and turned circles and danced for joy! His soldiers rushed out into the water to see this miracle!

This was so much more than just a physical healing. Naaman dipped himself—baptized himself—in the Jordan River, and his skin became as healthy as a young child's. This was a rebirth. Naaman took his entire party back to find Elisha, and when he found him, he proclaimed his newfound faith: "Now I know that there is no God in all the world except in Israel" (v. 15). Naaman asked permission to take a load of soil back to Aram so that he could make an altar and forever after sacrifice only to the Lord of Israel. And so, quite literally, Naaman brought the worship of the Lord of Israel to Aram.

This was so much more than just a physical healing.

We can only imagine what changes took place for the Aramean people because of our unnamed hero. Naaman would return home healthy, with a brand-new faith in the Lord of Israel, all thanks to her. And while the girl had acted selflessly, I imagine that life changed for her as well. But we'll never know. She isn't mentioned again. She's a perfect example of Tom Brokaw's definition of a hero: "Heroes are people who rise to the occasion and slip quietly away."[2]

A widely circulated proverb of anonymous origin reminds us that small things can have big results:

> *For want of a nail, the shoe was lost,*
> *For want of the shoe, the horse was lost,*
> *For want of the horse, the rider was lost,*
> *For want of the rider, the battle was lost,*
> *For want of the battle, the kingdom was lost,*
> *And all for the want of a nail!*[3]

Let's backtrack how faith in the one true God came to Aram through Naaman, the commander of the army. He believed because a prophet named Elisha healed him of his leprosy. Elisha offered to help after the king of Israel tore his robes in dismay. The king of Israel tore his robes because of a letter from the king of Aram, asking for the impossible. The king of Aram wrote the letter because Naaman asked permission to go to Israel, where a man could supposedly heal his leprosy. Naaman knew about the man because his wife's servant girl spoke up about him.

A man's life was forever changed. Faith came to a nation. All because a nameless slave girl did the unexpected. All because a nameless slave girl decided to "conquer evil by doing good" (Romans 12:21).

> Faith came to a nation. All because a
> nameless slave girl did the unexpected.

FOR THE PEOPLE WE MIGHT LEAST EXPECT

God sometimes prompts us to do the unexpected—and for the people we would least expect. It could be anybody.

In fact, before we go any further, would you take a moment to put yourself in this story? With you as the unnamed hero, who is the Naaman in your life?

Oh, you've got one. You have either someone in your life that you don't want to serve, or someone for whom you don't think it would make any difference. You probably have both. Be honest—nobody is looking over your shoulder right now. If God asks us to minister to people we'd least expect, then who is that for you?

Who would you have to first forgive before you could show him or her kindness? Maybe it's someone who has power over your life and has made things difficult or miserable for you. It could be your boss, your landlord, your professor. Is there somebody who's just a thorn in your side? A cantankerous neighbor, demanding client, stingy supplier, annoying coworker, competitive soccer mom, perfectionist supervisor, picky mother-in-law, fair-weather friend, old rival . . . you name it.

Jesus said: "To you who are willing to listen, I say, love your enemies! Do good to those who hate you. Bless those who curse you. Pray for those who hurt you" (Luke 6:27, 28).

Some of Jesus' commands are so contrary to what we'd expect, there can be a strong temptation to say, "Well, he couldn't have meant *that!* He must have meant . . ." But Jesus walked his talk like no one has since. Hanging from the nails, bleeding and gasping for breath to speak, he spent some of his final words saying, "Father, forgive them, for they don't know what they are doing" (Luke 23:34).

Some of Jesus' commands are so contrary to what we'd expect, there can be a strong temptation to say, "Well, he couldn't have meant *that!*"

Is there someone in your life whom, if you were honest, you truly do not expect ever to come to faith? You believe in a big God, and you know he sometimes does incredible things in people's lives. But if you were the betting sort, you wouldn't be putting your money on so-and-so having some life-changing experience. And you certainly wouldn't expect to be any part of it yourself.

Our expectations about people can completely blind us to God's work in their lives. God will have his way in the end, but our presumptions can keep us from seeing the heroic role he intends for us to play in it.

SEEING THROUGH EYES OF FAITH
It's important to ask ourselves the questions in those last several paragraphs, because answering them will begin to open a set of eyes inside us that,

unfortunately, tend to stay closed most of the time. Anticipating that our days and our lives will predictably unfold as expected, we are nearly blind to the incredible possibilities around us. These we can only see through the eyes of faith. The eyes in your head will see just your daily routine. The eyes of your *heart* can notice the unexpected opportunities you have to act on God's behalf.

Please don't read this the wrong way. The message of this unnamed hero's experience for us is *not* that we should forget our responsibilities and ignore our duties. Heroically doing the unexpected does not mean fudging the numbers, cheating on your wife, or quitting your job without a plan. No, that's how you become an unnamed *villain*. There's something deeply heroic about grinding it out, day after day, fulfilling your regular obligations and taking care of loved ones.

The eyes of your *heart* can notice the unexpected opportunities you have to act on God's behalf.

We have no idea how many days this unnamed girl worked in silence before the unexpected opportunity to speak came along. Though she was courageous to speak up, the moment itself would not have seemed extraordinary to anyone watching. Perhaps she had just finished washing the utensils after a meal, when she noticed Naaman's wife dabbing a tear. Maybe the girl was merely trying to offer some comfort. She certainly had no idea what a huge thing God was going to do through that seemingly unimportant, everyday moment. She simply said: "I wish my master would go to see the prophet in Samaria. He would heal him of his leprosy."

What if you did the same thing? What if you said:

- "I wish you'd come to get coffee with me and a friend of mine. She was in a situation just like yours, and I think it would encourage you so much to hear how she got through it."

- "I wish you'd try talking to God about that. I know it can feel strange and seem like a waste of time, especially if you're not used to it. But I'm telling you, he listens, and it helps."
- "I wish you'd come hear my pastor sometime. He's really down-to-earth—I think his messages would show you how to apply the Bible to your own life."
- "I wish you'd come check out the small group at my friend's place. It's just normal people trying to make some sense out of God and life. I really think it would help."

Or you could say, "I am going to kill you."

That's what a Philadelphia woman said to her son's murderer. Grieving the loss of her son, she sat through the trial and watched as the young thug was sentenced to prison. When the bailiff escorted the killer out of the courtroom, she delivered her own sentence: "When you get out, I am going to kill you."

Later, when the young man was released, she was there waiting for him. But something had changed. Time had healed much. She didn't curse him or threaten him. Instead, she asked if he needed a place to stay. He said that he did. She offered him a room in her house, and maybe because of her changed demeanor, or maybe because of the guilt he felt, he accepted.

She helped the young man get a job while he stayed with her. Gradually, his life stabilized. His time in prison and her unexpected kindness were changing him.

One day she came into his room to talk. "Do you remember when I said I was going to kill you?"

"How could I forget?" he replied.

"Well, I have already killed you," she said. "At least, I killed that thug that you used to be. Now he is dead and you are alive. So I did in fact kill you." She waited while this sank in. Then she said the unthinkable: "Now I would like to adopt you as my own son."

He accepted, and she adopted him. By doing the unexpected, this woman in Philadelphia turned her son's murderer into her own son. (Thanks to my friend Jade* from Cincinnati for sharing this story.)

"I have already killed you," she said. "At least, I killed that thug that you used to be."

What if I told you that God could influence the course of a nation with one sentence from your mouth? If you scoff, I'd like to suggest that the eyes of your soul are clamped shut. Open your eyes in faith to the possibilities, just as the slave girl did.

You don't need power or wealth. You don't need freedom. You don't even need a name.

You just need to do the unexpected.

---

*Friends submitted many of the stories in this book. Their names and stories are used with permission.

RELEASING **YOUR HEROIC** POTENTIAL

FOR INDIVIDUAL OR GROUP STUDY

1. Pretend that a major network is shooting a made-for-TV movie based on your life. It's one of those inspirational stories about an everyday hero. How would the actor who plays you in the movie approach your life? How would the hero (you) interact with his or her spouse, children, coworkers, and daily challenges?

2. Who is a Naaman in your life? Think about your neighbors, coworkers, relatives, supervisors, teachers, etc. Come up with at least one person— but preferably more than one. Now, one at a time, mentally identify with each one. What motivates them? What are they searching for? What pain are they experiencing? What is their greatest need?

3. Is there anything for which you need to forgive one of them? If so, what is it?

4. What role might God want you to play in reaching that person? Take a few moments to pray about this. What comes to mind? Could you imagine yourself stopping to chat for a few minutes, instead of just avoiding him or her? Is there something in particular you need to do for (or say to) the person when the opportunity presents itself? What is it?

5. How would expecting the *unexpected* change the way you spend time with God? If you believed in your bones that God was going to present you with opportunities today to do the unexpected, how would you pray differently? Be specific.

6. If doing something unexpected became normal living for you—if during *most* days you spoke up courageously or demonstrated unexpected kindness—how would that change the way you feel about your life?

DAILY STEPS TOWARD A HEROIC LIFE

- Think of a genuine compliment you can pay to a Naaman in your life. Nobody's *completely* rotten. Everyone has at least one good quality. Figure out what it is and point it out.

- Is there something for which you can genuinely thank your Naaman? He or she has probably done things that make you want to say "no thanks." But find something you *can* thank him for and do so—face-to-face or in a note.

- Pray for your Naaman. Don't just pray that God would fix him and show him how he's wrong. Pray for good things. Pray that God will bless him, give him joy, fulfill his dreams. If you can pray this way and mean it, you'll be amazed at what happens in your own heart.

- Before you leave the house or face your day, stop and ask God to open your eyes to the unexpected possibilities you will face. As this becomes a regular request, you will gradually begin to engage in the adventure amid your daily routine.

UNCLEAN

2 KINGS 7:3-11

God works through imperfect people.

Before we go any further, I need to come clean about something: I can be a hypocrite. As I wrote that last chapter, I really tried to take the message to heart. It's not easy.

For example, there's this guy who lives on our block in upper Manhattan. He stays up all hours of the night with his friends, hanging out in the street right outside our building. He drinks way too much and gets way too loud. Sometimes he sets off firecrackers right outside our window at three o'clock in the morning. Did I mention that he's a grown man? The police never arrive in time to catch him. The night that I opened the window and screamed, "Knock it off!" at the top of my lungs was not one of my finest moments.

One night, as I was in the middle of writing that last chapter, I turned to my wife and (trying to repress my anger) said, "He's *my* Naaman." And it occurred to me that I had to do the unexpected and try to build a relationship with this guy.

My next thought was that it would be easier to rewrite the last chapter instead . . . and I actually considered doing it. It would be funny if it weren't so true.

"GOOD" COMPANY

If at this point you're not exactly feeling like a saint—if reading about the unnamed slave girl's amazing gesture of forgiveness has left you feeling a little less-than-the-perfect Christian—then you are in good company. Well . . . maybe not *good* company. But you've *got* company.

Maybe for you it's not a forgiveness issue—but we've all got issues. We've all done things we regret. And what can be more disheartening, we all face an ongoing struggle with shortcomings. We judge. We envy. We gossip. We lust. Given a choice to serve ourselves or someone else, whom do we usually choose? You've got to look out for number one, don't you? Everyday life reveals each of us to be fundamentally selfish. All of us, every last one, have missed the mark. We "all have sinned and fall short of the glory of God" (Romans 3:23, *NIV*). Each of us has chosen—a thousand times—to be the villain instead of the hero.

Each of us has chosen—a thousand times—
to be the villain instead of the hero.

You may consider yourself so broken and dirty that you doubt God would ever use you for much, if at all. These feelings of shame can have the effect of a nerve toxin that paralyzes your heroic impulse. If you'll pardon the superhero metaphor, shame is the Christian's kryptonite. Sometimes we want to do the right thing, but shame freezes us with doubt. Sometimes we *don't* want to do the right thing, and shame provides the perfect excuse for us to sit on our hands.

It is so important that you read about our next unnamed hero. He*roes*, actually—there were four of them. These four were far from perfect, in more ways than one. And yet, God made them heroes. They celebrated victory over an entire army and saved an entire city. In a weird way, God actually used their weakness to accomplish his will.

If you don't know it already, your sin—your brokenness, weakness, selfishness, uncleanness—cannot keep you from acting heroically on God's behalf. There are consequences to sin, sure, but grace is deeper still. Everyone has sinned, both heroes and villains. The truth is that God only uses imperfect people.

THE LESSER OF TWO EVILS

Naaman's dramatic conversion (in chapter 1) didn't end the hostilities between the Arameans and Israelites. In 2 Kings 6, the king of Aram mustered his forces and invaded Samaria, surrounding the city and choking off supplies. Terrible famine developed within. People scrounged the last bits of food, and starvation tightened its stranglehold on the city's inhabitants. The siege lasted so long that a donkey's head sold for about two pounds of silver, an exorbitant price. It's difficult for us today to imagine how dire things can become during the final death throes of famine. Mothers, in ravenous mania, ate their own children (vv. 26-30).

Enter four of the unlikeliest heroes you could imagine. "Now there were four men with leprosy sitting at the entrance of the city gates" (2 Kings 7:3). In that day the prescription for people suffering with leprosy was severe. They were quarantined, and in order to protect other Israelites from being contaminated, they were supposed to cover the lower part of their faces and cry out "Unclean! Unclean!" (Leviticus 13:45, 46). These four men had survived by begging food from the people who had cast them out—the people who were now themselves starving to death.

As their story unfolds across the pages of Scripture, we find them caught in a dilemma. "We will starve if we stay here, but with the famine in the city, we will starve if we go back there," they reasoned (2 Kings 7:4). They had a decision to make. If they decided to go into the city, they would starve to death. But if they chose to stay where they were, they would also starve to death. If they tried to leave the city, enemies might slaughter them, and they might starve to death anyway. They had to choose between certain death and probable death. "So we might as well go out and surrender to the Aramean army. If they let us live, so much the better. But if they kill us, we would have died anyway" (v. 4). This decision to take their chances with the Arameans would put them precisely in the right place at the right time to be heroes for God. I doubt they had the slightest suspicion that they had been singled out by God to save the day.

Before we look at what happened, I want to point something out: If God wants to use us for some heroic act, he is able to put us in the right place at the right time—even if we're unaware of it. It's important to realize this in order to begin believing that God really can make heroes out of "unclean" people. We each have the freedom to choose how to think, speak, and act, but God is so much wiser than we are. If he wants to, he can play us like a fiddle. If God wants to position you for some good work, he can do it.

They had to choose between certain death and probable death.

A friend of mine found this out firsthand when he decided to take the "scenic route" home. For seemingly no reason, he drove a much longer route that curved around a lake. When he looked over at the water, he saw something sticking out of the surface that did not belong: taillights. He noticed a couple of elderly people at the shore, frantically shouting in his direction. He yanked the wheel to the right, stomped on the brake, and jumped out.

A gentleman who appeared to be in his nineties was pointing toward the floating car and shouting, "We have to get her! She's still in there!"

We?! he thought, privately amused. *There's no way either of these two is gonna be able to get her.* Impulsively, he removed his wallet and splashed out toward the sinking car.

When he pried the driver side door open, he found an elderly lady with her seat belt on, clasping the wheel at ten o'clock and two o'clock. After several moments of effort, he managed to maneuver her out into the water and toward the shore. He carried her over some very rough rocks and up onto the grass. Then they watched in horror as the front end of the car tipped forward. It sank unceremoniously, leaving behind only a ring of ripples and foam.

My friend later discovered that the lake dropped off near the center to a depth of sixty feet.

> I doubt that the four outcasts were aware that
> God was putting them right where he wanted them.

The damsel in distress was eighty-seven years old. Once her ninety-three-year-old husband knew that she was safe, he was pretty upset about the car (and her driving!). My friend slipped away home to clean off the muck from the lake. Later, when the story broke on the five o'clock news, the anchor asked if anyone could supply the identity of the "mystery hero" who left before anyone could learn his name.

Looking back, my friend is certain that, even though he was completely unaware of it, the Holy Spirit guided him to take the long way home that day. He had never before taken that route.

FROM OUTCASTS TO CONQUERORS

I doubt that the four outcasts were aware that God was putting them right where he wanted them. They waited until twilight before setting out toward the Aramean camp, maybe to travel undetected, or perhaps hoping the darkness would conceal their infected skin. Much to their surprise, "when they came to the edge of the camp, no one was there!" (v. 5). They entered a ghost town of abandoned tents and equipment. Horses and donkeys stood tethered to posts. Fires smoldered. I imagine them tiptoeing in among the tents, cautiously investigating. Apparently, the Aramean warriors had just up and left—and left everything!

What the four didn't know was that earlier in the night, before they arrived, "the Lord had caused the Aramean army to hear the clatter of speeding chariots and the galloping of horses and the sounds of a great army approaching" (v. 6). The Arameans, reasoning that the Israelites had hired Hittite and Egyptian mercenaries, panicked and fled wildly into the night.

I need to hit the pause button again. I don't know what you are facing or what difficult thing the Lord may have asked you to do, or *will* ask you to do in the future. Whatever it is, be assured: God can accomplish it. Sometimes he chooses not to, and that's a whole other book. Be assured that he can, though, and that he doesn't need you to do it. He doesn't need anybody. He can beat an army with a soundtrack.

Whatever it is, be assured: God can accomplish it.

Now back to our story.

So the men with leprosy arrived at the edge of camp, starving and most likely praying that God would show them favor among their enemies, only to find the entire camp abandoned. After they pinched themselves and probably laughed out loud, they went from tent to tent, eating and drinking. I imagine they timidly drew the flaps of the first tent aside and discovered, illuminated by the soft flickering of lamplight, a table set for the evening meal with steaming lamb chops, golden-brown loaves of bread, wooden bowls mounded with figs and olives, cups topped with bright red wine. Not caring whether this was a dream or not, they rushed the table and stuffed their faces. They threw their heads back and laughed with their mouths full, slapped each other on the back, and licked grease off their fingers. They lifted cups with both hands, drained them, and chortled as the wine dribbled down their chins.

Our four unnamed heroes did what I think any of us would do, given the circumstances. They helped themselves. Then, once they had their fill, they started carrying off gold, silver, and clothing and hid it outside the camp. The Scripture says that they "went into one tent after another" (v. 8).

Now, wait a minute. Granted, they hadn't been warmly embraced by their people back home, but the famine there was so severe that mothers were eating their children. Meanwhile, here they were, partying into the wee hours of the morning. It's one thing, as the flight attendant advises just before takeoff, to put your own oxygen mask on before you try to help someone else. This was something different. Our four unclean heroes cleaned out a tent of all its valuables, went and found a place to hide it all, and then returned and cleaned out another tent. Who knows how long this went on.

At some point their consciences finally spoke up louder than their self-interest, and they said to one another, "This is not right. This is a day of good news, and we aren't sharing it with anyone!" (v. 9). Even then, though, their motivations were a bit less than purely altruistic, for they reasoned, "If we wait until morning, some calamity will certainly fall upon us. Come on, let's go back and tell the people at the palace" (v. 9). Their behavior reveals a basic self-centeredness. Self-preservation had driven them to the Aramean camp. There they bumbled into a victory that they had nothing to do with, and greedily gobbled up the spoils. They even hoarded some for later before thinking to share with their starving neighbors. Only the fear of retribution from the Lord finally compelled them to return. These four were unclean in more ways than one.

I don't want to be too hard on them, because life had obviously handed them a pretty rough deal. And to be fair, they didn't have to go back and share anything. They could have taken the goods and run off. After all, why should they help a people who had cast them out? That said, surely someone from the city had shown them kindness. They were still alive, so someone must have taken care of them. Regardless, the results of the famine were so grotesque that you wouldn't wish it on your worst enemy. Although these heroes eventually did the right thing, they were far from ideal.

ALL OF US

True confession: I love these guys. I get a kick out of them, I think, because I have so much in common with them. I don't have leprosy, thank God, but I do share their uncleanness in a deeper sense. I think we all do. Sin is essentially selfishness, and aren't we all fundamentally self-centered? Aren't we all unclean, in one way or another?

The Bible certainly says so. "All of us have become like one who is unclean, and all our righteous acts are like filthy rags" (Isaiah 64:6, *NIV*). *All of us* have become unclean. Even our *righteous* acts are compared to filthy rags. Each of us was raised in a world hopelessly marred by sin. Each of us contributed to the brokenness by making our own sinful decisions. The world wallows in the sickness of sin, and we are infected by its muck and filth. Our attempts to cover up are like putting on grimy rags—even our righteous acts are tainted with impure motives.

The world wallows in the sickness of sin, and we are infected by its muck and filth. Our attempts to cover up are like putting on grimy rags.

Have you watched the nightly news lately? It's grim.

Or skim through the rest of 2 Kings and notice how many good, well-intentioned kings fell into idolatry and sin toward the end of their lives. This has been the case with all of God's heroes, whether the Scripture records their names or not. Some of the greatest heroes in the Bible committed some of the most heinous sins. Moses was a murderer. King David was an adulterer. Solomon, the wisest man in his day, succumbed to idolatry and in his old age worshipped some of the gods of his foreign wives and concubines. You read that right: wives (plural) *and* concubines, hundreds of them. Matthew was a shady tax collector. Mary Magdalene was infested with seven demons. Paul had supervised the murder of Christians.

God can transform the dirtiest of us into one of his heroes.

New York Yankee great Mickey Mantle (who battled alcoholism most of his life) revealed a deep understanding of the human condition when he said, "You never have to wait long, or look far, to be reminded of how thin the line is between being a hero or a goat."[1]

But if the problem is a dark shadow, then God responds with the sun. If the problem is a festering sore, then God's answer is an ocean of cleansing water. The good news is really that good.

God can transform the dirtiest of us into one of his heroes. Take a look at Jesus' genealogy in the first chapter of Matthew, and you'll find that among his ancestors are Judah, who committed incest with Tamar, and Rahab, who was a prostitute. If God can literally bring the sinless one through the bloodline of these broken people, can't he work through you?

I love these four outcasts because I identify with their sinfulness and selfishness. But God loved them so much more—and he knew their potential. When the four outcasts finally came to their moral senses, they returned to share the good news with their countrymen. They explained to the gatekeepers of the city that the Aramean soldiers had disappeared, leaving all of their supplies behind. "Then the gatekeepers shouted the news to the people in the palace" (2 Kings 7:11). Before, people probably had ignored these men, perhaps tossed a crust of bread or a coin as they hurried past. Now their words were shouted to the people in the palace!

None of our shortcomings disqualify us from God's redemptive work. In fact, sometimes it's through our weakness that God works most powerfully. The apostle Paul learned this after he begged God on three separate occasions to heal him of a physical infirmity (the Bible doesn't share the specifics about what was wrong). God's response to him was, "My grace is sufficient for you, for my power is made perfect in weakness" (2 Corinthians 12:9, *NIV*).

These four unclean heroes prove that none of us can use our brokenness as an excuse not to serve him.

This was certainly true for our four unnamed heroes. The fact that they were outcasts at the entrance to the city, rather than being trapped inside, actually positioned them to be sent on this mission. God's power was made perfect in their weakness—it couldn't have been clearer who really defeated the Arameans.

There are two edges to this message: 1) It's encouraging to know that God uses unclean people to do the heroic. You need never feel that your sin, your past, or your imperfections will keep you from being powerfully used by God. 2) The other edge is sharp. These four unclean heroes prove that none of us can use our brokenness as an excuse not to serve him. No more dismissing your responsibility to act heroically with a bunch of woe-is-me-I'm-nothing-but-a-sinner talk. That reasoning won't stand up against the truth. No more sitting on your hands. Jesus was perfect, but when he returned to Heaven—it sounds preposterous, but it's true—he left *us* to do his work. You and me, with all of our foolishness and sin.

UNCLEAN BUT CLEANSED

I recently had an experience that etched this truth into my soul, reminding me both of my own uncleanness and of God's ability to work through me regardless. One Sunday morning at worship, during the "meet and greet" time, I turned around and behind me was a large, scary-looking dude with a long goatee and a huge tattoo of a human skull on his forearm.

I said, "I like your tattoo." On closer inspection, I discovered that the skull was formed out of the figures of naked women. As we chatted, I learned that the image was a recreation of a famous painting by Salvador Dali. It seemed there was a little more to this guy than met the eye.

I found out that he was in town only for a few months, helping a family through a difficult situation. Attending a worship service was an unusual thing for him to do. Thinking about how bored and lonely he must be in New York City away from his friends and job, I invited him to hang out sometime. A little to my surprise, he was interested, and we made tentative plans to go check out a park near my place. I had a strong sense that God was doing something important in this guy's life.

Fast-forward to the evening when we were supposed to hang out, and my selfish side had taken over. Sure, I had had a difficult day at work and not much sleep the night before, but really, I was just being selfish. I wanted to put my feet up and tune out. My Sunday-morning concern for the man's loneliness had dissolved during the workweek. I still had a strong sense that God was up to something, but I just didn't care. I decided not to call him—and hoped he wouldn't call me.

Looking back, I'm embarrassed by how close I came to missing out.

Fast-forward to the evening when we were supposed
to hang out, and my selfish side had taken over.

Fortunately, he contacted me, and I begrudgingly agreed to get together. I downed a cup of coffee and walked to the park. When we met, our conversation—for whatever reason—went very deep, very fast. He soon told me something important about himself. He told me that he was a fugitive.

You read that right.

He had a long history of dealing drugs and of violence. He had been in and out of prison and was currently in violation of his parole, with a warrant for his arrest awaiting him should he ever return to his home state. For the first time in many years, he had been sober for a couple of months. He was attending worship and reading the Bible. And he was convinced that he needed to return home and turn himself in. He wanted to serve his time and be done with it. His former suppliers and distributors thought he was crazy. A few tried to understand, but most mocked him, and some tried to drag him back into their lifestyle.

He was convinced of what he had to do.

There's a Bible term for that: it's called repentance. I couldn't believe what an about-face this guy was contemplating, and I told him that I believed God was at work in his life. We talked for another hour or so. We talked about grace and what Christ came to accomplish. It became clear that he really wanted to give his life back to God. So I asked him simply, "Do you want to give your life to God?"

He said, "Yes . . ." but then hesitated, and repeated, "Yes."

"Why did you hesitate?" I asked him. He explained that he didn't think he could, because of some of the things he had done.

And there it was: uncleanness. We're all stuck in it, aren't we?

I told him how normal it was to feel that way. Maybe some of the things he had done were particularly ugly, but so were some of the things I had done. Becoming a Christ follower isn't about being clean; it's about being *cleansed*. I told him two or three of the things that I'd done that I'm most embarrassed by (I've finally accepted God's grace to the point where I can talk about some of these things without cringing). Then I told him how close I had come to calling off our meeting. Here he was, on the brink of perhaps the most important decision of his life, and I had been almost too selfish to give a couple of hours. The grace you receive when you give your life to Christ, you continue to receive for all of your shortcomings thereafter.

When it was clear that he understood this amazing gift of grace, I asked him again if he wanted to turn his life over to God. He asked how. We talked about repentance, faith, confession, and baptism. I met with him regularly, talking about the Bible, sharing books with him . . . and we prayed for one another.

Becoming a Christ follower isn't about being clean; it's about being *cleansed*.

When I baptized him, I couldn't believe how close I had come to missing out on such a huge moment—and on finding such a good friend. I love that guy.

My friend returned to his home state and turned himself in. We've kept in touch, and it's amazing to hear how God is transforming this man. He reads his Bible so often that some of the other inmates have begun to call him Bible Boy and have tried to pick on him. He's a pretty big guy, so I'm not too worried about him physically. But to keep from returning to his former life of violence, he's trying to avoid arguing and fighting altogether.

He has begun to reach out to the young man who sleeps in the next bunk. "I swear he's me when I was eighteen," my friend wrote. "When I ask him about Jesus, he answers the same way I used to when I was young. He says he used to believe but that he gave it up because he thought he wasn't worth being saved."

It can be so difficult to believe that God wants to accept us, as unclean as we are. I find the transforming power of God's love and forgiveness more impressive than even his great miracles. Sure, it's amazing when God conquers an army without shedding any blood. But what other god can take a violent man and turn him into a man who resists violence? What other god transforms a criminal into a man who shows criminals another way? Only the God of the Bible works so powerfully through unclean people.

RELEASING YOUR HEROIC POTENTIAL

FOR INDIVIDUAL OR GROUP STUDY

1. Who did you admire when you were growing up? Why? Was he or she perfect? If not, what were that person's shortcomings?

2. If you could change one thing about yourself, what would you change? Why?

3. When you think about doing the heroic, do any of your weaknesses or shortcomings cause you to doubt that God would use you? What practical steps can you take to get beyond those excuses?

4. Has God ever used your weaknesses for a good purpose? In what ways have your struggles given you understanding, or made it easier for people to relate to you?

5. If you have given your life to Christ, then hopefully, you understand that you have been forgiven by God. Do you *feel* forgiven (clean)? If not, why not?

DAILY STEPS TOWARD A HEROIC LIFE

- When you pray, thank God for his grace. If you are in Christ, then you *are* forgiven. Simply thank him for it. As you practice this gratitude, it will transform your heart.

- Make a list of the specific sins or shortcomings that are a source of guilt or shame for you. Thank God for his forgiveness of each one. Read Romans 8:1 (in several different Bible translations) and believe it. Then throw the list away. Better yet, burn it.

- If you have something from your past or something with which you currently struggle that is an ongoing source of shame, find someone with whom you can confess it. Choose someone gentle and mature whom you can trust to keep a confidence. You will be amazed at the healing that comes through confession (see James 5:16).

- Read Psalm 103. Even better, memorize it. Move at your own pace, really chewing on the words and allowing its truth to change your heart.

THREE

UNPOLISHED
LUKE 2:1-20

The power is in the message, not the messenger.

ction movies used to make me feel like I could be a hero. The action was about a normal guy who was thrust, against his wishes, into extraordinary circumstances. By courage and perseverance and a lot of luck, he somehow managed to come out on top. Those films left me feeling inspired that if a similar scenario should ever happen to me, then maybe, just maybe, I'd have what it takes.

The newer films don't have quite the same effect. They're much more entertaining, but something is wrong. They've got it all backwards. Today's heroes are amazingly well trained. They have secret backgrounds in special forces or as government assassins. They speak fourteen languages fluently. They know how to diffuse bombs, operate aircraft, and perform minor surgery on . . . *themselves*!

During one of these films, there is almost always a moment when I think, *Yup, that's when I would have died. I have no idea how to short-circuit a switch box to make the train jump onto a different track. I don't have what it takes to be* that *hero.*

WHAT YOU CANNOT DO

Inadequacy could be called shame's nasty little brother. It can sidle up beside you anytime, anywhere, teasing and belittling. I've felt it even in worship. One time as I listened to a young church planter give a brilliant message—he must have read seven books in preparation for it—I thought, *It takes me two weeks to get through a paperback. I could never lead a church in Manhattan.* The feeling wasn't logical, but it was real.

The heroic acts of other people sometimes have an effect on us that's the opposite of the effect they should have. Instead of feeling empowered and capable, we sometimes wilt.

- "I could never adopt a kid with those physical disabilities."
- "I could never live there."
- "If I were in that situation, I'd have no idea what to say."

I'm sure you can relate. Even the most confident among us sometimes entertain the idea that we don't have what it takes. And in no situation is this truer than when it comes to sharing our faith with others. Most of us feel completely inadequate to communicate our faith. Surely we need special training to be able to do it well. We want to share some good news, but we don't know how—and we definitely don't want to push people away. We're understandably gun-shy, perhaps because we've witnessed some bizarre attempts at faith sharing that involved a lot of unasked-for advice, threats, and pressure to make a decision *right now.*

It's normal to feel some trepidation. You may have experienced that in the course of reading this book. Maybe reading about my new friend at the end of the last chapter left you feeling a little unpolished. Perhaps you thought to yourself, *Sure, Chris, you had the right answers—you've worked as a pastor! You've received training at a seminary. I wouldn't know how to explain my faith in a situation like that. God would never use me in that way.*

John Wooden, the first person honored in the Naismith Memorial Basketball Hall of Fame as both a player and a coach, gave some appropriate advice: "Do not let what you cannot do interfere with what you can do."[1]

People are still hungry for truth. Sharp pangs for it gnaw in the guts of their souls. If you can offer even the tiniest morsel of real truth—something that's true both theologically and to you experientially—you'll find that the message is often much more welcome than you think. It is *good* news, after all.

The heroic acts of other people sometimes have an effect on us that's the opposite of the effect they should have. Instead of feeling empowered and capable, we sometimes wilt.

So I suggest that the older movies are truer. Becoming a hero doesn't call for any special skills. You don't need to know how to make a bomb out of last night's leftovers. Life doesn't call for a larger-than-life hero—life-size will do just fine, if we're willing to try.

In no circumstance is this more the case than when sharing faith. In fact, I think that we've entered an era in our culture when the more polished, well-trained evangelist may not necessarily be the hero with the power to switch on spiritual lightbulbs. When it comes to the people you know who are not yet Christian, you are the most qualified person to share the good news with them. Much more important than having the wording all perfectly worked out is the relational capital you have with them that will enable them to trust your intentions. Untrained and unpolished—but utterly genuine—people, simply prepared to gently and respectfully talk about their relationship with God, will best connect with people today.

But this isn't new. God has been communicating his love through untrained people for thousands of years. There is actually freedom in our feelings of inadequacy, if you'll read on to discover it. You can relax, because it never did depend on the messenger. God demonstrated this over two thousand years ago, when he picked ordinary, unpolished men to share the news about the most significant cosmic event in the history of our planet.

THE LEAST LIKELY MESSENGERS

There were a group of shepherds watching over their flocks near Bethlehem as that first Christmas approached. These men were important to society. People depended on the wool they harvested, and in some cases on the meat and dairy. Their labors clothed and fed the community. They were simultaneously removed from society though. They lived simply, passing silent hours, watching their flocks nibble the green grass, their gaze as steady as the noonday sun. Their minds quietly calculated how long before need would compel them toward fresh pasture, and where they should seek it. Neither their thoughts nor their flocks could ever stray far from water. At shearing time, they would sell the wool to merchants and at markets. Mostly, the shepherds lived in the field with their animals.

When Augustus, the mighty emperor of Rome, called for the census that would send Jewish people from one end of the land to the other to register in the cities of their ancestry, I doubt these men concerned themselves much with the bustle. They knew precisely the number of sheep in their care, which ones were pregnant, and when they should expect to be naming the newborn lambs. But they knew nothing of the Lamb of God, who rode peacefully within his mother toward Bethlehem.

At night the shepherds—earthy men who smelled of beast and field— slept among their flocks. Sometimes they sat and watched, silent figures silhouetted by the heavenly splash of sparkling stars. When they slept, it was always with one ear ready to respond to any bleating that warned of a nearby predator. When danger did come, a shepherd's grip tightened around his staff, and the shepherd's crook became a cudgel.

Little did they know that not far off, Joseph guided his young fiancée away from the overcrowded inn and sought a place for her to give birth. The God who created the universe and everything in it entered the world humbly and quietly. His mother wrapped his fragile limbs in cloth and laid him in the only crib available—a feeding trough. The shepherds sat underneath the glow of the stars that he created, and would never have known that their God lay cooing nearby, if something extraordinary hadn't happened.

"Suddenly, an angel of the Lord appeared among them, and the radiance of the Lord's glory surrounded them" (Luke 2:9). One moment the shepherds were in quiet darkness; only the occasional grunt of slumbering sheep and the whisper of the cool night breeze over the field ever broke the stillness. The next moment a mighty being of piercing light burst forth from the night, and they were flooded with the heavenly brilliance of God's glory. They were, as any of us would be, in a word—terrified!

The shepherds sat underneath the glow of the stars that he created, and would never have known that their God lay cooing nearby, if something extraordinary hadn't happened.

But the angel reassured them. "'Don't be afraid!' he said. 'I bring you good news that will bring great joy to all people. The Savior—yes, the Messiah, the Lord—has been born today in Bethlehem, the city of David! And you will recognize him by this sign: You will find a baby wrapped snugly in strips of cloth, lying in a manger'" (vv. 10-12). Then a vast host of other angelic beings appeared—the "armies of heaven," the Scripture calls them—praising God together, crying in unison, "Glory to God in the highest heaven, and peace on earth to those with whom God is pleased" (vv. 13, 14). Then they departed, leaving the shepherds stunned, their hearts pounding in their throats.

"Let's go to Bethlehem!" the shepherds exclaimed. "Let's see this thing that has happened, which the Lord has told us about" (v. 15). They left their flocks and hurried off to the village, where they found Mary and Joseph and, just as they were told, the baby lying in the manger. They were so moved by his presence and by the fulfillment of the angel's words that before they returned to their flocks, they did something interesting. They spread the word. The text says that they "told everyone what had happened and what the angel had said to them about this child" (v. 17).

Of all the people sleeping nearby on the night when Jesus was born, the heavenly host appeared to a group of men sleeping outdoors with their animals. The angels could have commissioned any of the rhetoricians, philosophers, or religious leaders. They could have enlisted powerful politicians with speechwriters at their disposal. Instead, they appeared to untrained men of the field—not the most likely messengers.

What's even more interesting is how people responded to their message. Luke 2:18 records that "all who heard the shepherds' story were astonished."

AN ASTONISHING MESSAGE

The people were deeply affected by the shepherds' story. I find this so interesting because I'd guarantee that they were not the most eloquent public speakers. To sheep, they were poets, sure, perhaps some of them even great singers. They had generations-old calls and trills and ways of clicking their tongues that would tell sheep to be alert, to stay close, to come to them. But the shepherds spent much more time speaking with animals than with people. I doubt seriously that they were very well-spoken. Yet everyone who heard them was *astonished*.

There's a principle at work here that is so simple, it would be easy to overlook. That would be a mistake because this principle can dispel our feelings of inadequacy about sharing our faith. The people were astonished, quite simply, because the power was in the message, not the messenger.

It wasn't the only time in the Bible that people would be astonished by the words of untrained men. Later, after Jesus' death and resurrection, Peter and John had the opportunity to speak before the Sanhedrin, the council of priests. Acts 4:13 records that "when they saw the courage of Peter and John and realized that they were unschooled, ordinary men, they were astonished and they took note that these men had been with Jesus" (*NIV*).

It's the same today. God has entrusted us with an astonishing message. Unfortunately, it's easy for us to lose sight of how amazing God's plan to save us really is. Every time I get the opportunity to communicate any part of this incredible reality to someone who is new to it, I'm reminded by people's reaction just how unique and wonderful it is. The world, which operates on a performance-based value system, never saw it coming. No longer must we perform, pay back, or make amends. No longer must we offer sacrifices in the futile attempt to make up for our sins. And no longer is our standing with God dependent on our obedience to religious ritual and law.

It seems too good to be true. There must be some kind of catch. But in an astonishing act of love, the God who *is love* paid the price for us once and for all. The innocent died on behalf of the guilty. What does he ask from each of us? Believe him. Trust him. Turn away from self, and let his acceptance and love softly change you from the inside out.

Life with this God is like a never-ending sense of relief.

Life with this God is like a never-ending sense of relief.

At this point, you may be tempted to think, *Sure, the day the armies of Heaven appear to me and give me special instructions to go and witness a miracle, I'll go tell everyone about it too.* Of course, God's work in our lives is seldom that dramatic. It is nonetheless real. Each of us has a story to share. Just ask Christian people, "How has God changed your life?" and you will get a unique answer from each. Some will talk about despair turned into joy. Others will talk about ongoing depression, and how God has taught them patience and trust through it. Some will speak of anger that has turned into peace, bitterness into forgiveness, loneliness into acceptance. Each of us has an astonishing story to share.

All that is required of you to share it with another is willingness and natural sincerity. No polish needed. The message has the power to draw people closer to God. Only the legalistically religious are hardened by it. All others take a step toward faith when they hear it. Even people who refuse to accept it often gain a softer disposition toward God. Those who accept the fact that they cannot and do not have to earn their place with him find that living with this message of grace has the power to transform their lives. Grace moves people toward godliness in ways that guilt, pressure, and human effort never could.

But we forget. Some of us grow bored with the Scripture, absently munch the Communion emblems, and no longer hear the good news as a reality, but only as words. These are symptoms of a dangerously drying faith. The gospel is so much more than just being saved from Hell and then going about your business. Accepting Christ's gift initiates a complete restoration of the glory for which we were originally intended. God brings us freedom, healing, wholeness, and all the heavenly blessings. He gives joy and peace. He gives us purpose. If we aren't experiencing subtle changes in our lives and hearts, then our faith is either wilting or we're not paying attention.

Sometimes we can be reluctant to share about our faith because we have little to share.

PREPARED, NOT POLISHED

First Peter 3:15 says, "Always be prepared to give an answer to everyone who asks you to give the reason for the hope that you have. But do this with gentleness and respect" (*NIV*). People around us struggle with all the same things in life that we do, and have many of our same hopes and dreams. We each have opportunities from time to time to share something about how we've seen God at work in our lives. If we prioritize relationships and are prepared to speak gently and respectfully, the opportunities come up even more often.

Mark Twain admitted that "it usually takes more than three weeks to prepare a good impromptu speech."[2] Of course, he was being tongue-in-cheek, but there is some truth to his words. Often, the difference between those who share their faith and those who don't is simple preparedness. This is not to be confused with special training in some kind of "method" of evangelism. It's simply a matter of being thoughtful about our faith. Think about what life was like before you placed your trust in God, about what was missing. Recall the reasons you decided to believe and turn toward him. Make it a practice to reflect on how he has changed and *is* changing your life.

> ## No one is better qualified to share how God has impacted your life than you are.

Eloquence isn't the issue here. We don't have to worry so much about exactly what to say, or how to say it. We just need to be genuine and available to talk about what we've experienced. No one is better qualified to share how God has impacted your life than you are. Each of us can be more intentional about building relationships. When we do, conversation about God naturally occurs. Each of us has some key circumstances—whether our office softball team, kids' soccer games, or study group—that will gradually provide opportunities to share our faith. We just have to be sincere and natural about what we believe. I think we need to be much more intentional about sharing our faith than we tend to be. But we need to do it all above the table, so to speak. People's hearts are very important to God, and we must handle them with care. When you talk about your faith:

- Don't try to angle people.
- Don't try to manipulate people.
- Don't try to scare or pressure people.
- Don't try to subtly shift the conversation.
- Either be direct, or wait until you can be.

People appreciate gentle, respectful directness. This doesn't require any special training in tactical weapons, or a superhero utility belt or cape, just some basic sensitivity. When your focus is on the person and the relationship, everything else sort of falls into place. You have a powerful message to share about how God has changed your life. People are hungry for something real. When they see a professional Christian speaker (live or on TV) who seems to have it all together, they may close up, thinking it unlikely that this "polished" guy has ever known any real trouble or could understand their day-to-day situations. Some might even think he's a complete fake.

A friend you care about might come to worship or a small group with you, and draw closer to God that way. That's great. Many won't. Even those who do so will have questions and doubts and need some explanation from someone close to them.

So it comes down to you. If you don't share faith with them, who will?

REASON TO HOPE

I know a young lady who has mitochondrial myopathy, a disease that attacks the mitochondria, the energy "factories" inside our cells. Let's call her Janet. Her case wreaks havoc on a number of different body systems, impairing the function of many of her muscles, so she is confined to a wheelchair and depends heavily on nursing staff for her survival. Her mind is as sharp as ever but is trapped inside a damaged body. Her case is pretty severe—she was supposed to die more than a year ago.

I have lost track of how many people she has encouraged toward faith in Christ. One of her staff started attending church with her, and his faith was rekindled. Another began to attend church with Janet initially because she had to, but now, after all the conversations they've had about faith, this young lady goes by herself even when Janet is too sick to go. One day Janet ran into one of her high school teachers, and the two had much to talk about. During the conversation about Janet's illness, they spoke a lot about faith, and Janet's teacher has been coming to church with her ever since.

Janet maintained a friendship with a young man from college who struggled to believe. Bit by bit, conversation after conversation, he gradually felt more accepted by God. He decided to be baptized. At one point, she met another young man who suffered from cerebral palsy. "People don't take him seriously," she told me. *She* did though, understanding full well what it was to command a broken body with a whole mind. Over time, her faith rubbed off on him, and he too decided to be baptized. She knew another person who suffered from cerebral palsy, a young woman. In the course of their friendship, Janet started talking to her about her faith, and invited her to come to her small group. Once again, over time, this young woman too began to believe, and decided to be baptized.

I have lost track of how many people she
has encouraged toward faith in Christ.

Now, Janet would be the first to admit that she is far from perfect. And talk about unpolished! Because of her illness, she has to concentrate just to articulate, and it can be difficult to understand her. Some of the medication she was on produced the nasty side effect of periodic vomiting. She had to have a bucket with her at all times. And because she knows how short her time may be, she has a tendency to be pretty direct with her words (which can come across as either refreshingly straightforward, or a little blunt, depending on the circumstances). So I was on the edge of my seat when I asked her how she helped all these people come to faith.

She said, simply, "I just try to share with everyone I meet." When I prodded, I learned that her faith tended to come up very naturally in conversation. For example, Janet likes to paint, and when friends would ask her about the inspiration behind a certain painting, Janet's response would naturally include something about her relationship with God. At one point, she said, "Sometimes, here in my wheelchair, not being able to hold a job down, I feel like I'm not doing much with my life. But these relationships let me know that I'm making a difference."

Relationships. It's so simple, so natural . . . it seems like it should be more complicated than that. It isn't. Just be yourself and prioritize relationships. Don't try to seem more religious than you are, but don't be any less either. Be sensitive and respectful, but don't be ashamed. Care genuinely for those around you—and be yourself.

What if we all started to get this right? Imagine the countless little God-breathed conversations, if God's people were ready to give reasons for their hope. Imagine the countless nudges people would experience toward faith, if we all tended to our relationships the way the shepherds outside of Bethlehem tended to the needs of their sheep. Imagine millions of unpolished, everyday heroes who care more about people than about their own image; who are genuine, but gentle; ready to speak, but respectful.

> What if we all started to get this right? Imagine the countless little God-breathed conversations, if God's people were ready to give reasons for their hope.

People you know are experiencing so much emotional pain from doubt, worry, guilt, and the fear of death, and you can offer relief. Life can be brutal. Most people just get knocked around, make tons of mistakes, and live with a gnawing fear that death is coming and God is angry. Others are doing pretty well, but struggle with the nagging emptiness that there must be more to life. Without God, hope can be so fleeting. Most people want to hope. Some people want to believe, but are afraid of what God may be like, or of how he might feel toward them. That's where you come in.

You can give people reason to hope . . . because the power is in the message.

RELEASING **YOUR HEROIC** POTENTIAL

FOR INDIVIDUAL OR GROUP STUDY

1. What was life like for you before you believed in Christ? What things were difficult? What was missing?

2. What prompted you to accept what Jesus did? How did you become a Christian?

3. How has your life changed through your relationship with God? Has anything gotten easier? If so, what is it? What things have gotten more challenging? How have *you* changed?

4. What has God been teaching you lately?

5. In which areas of your life do you regularly interact with people who have not yet begun to trust Jesus? Have you considered your testimony too "unpolished" to share with them?

6. What changes could you make to your priorities or lifestyle in order to have more face time with people who are farther away from God?

DAILY STEPS TOWARD A HEROIC LIFE

- Identify a few people who are close to you but far from God, and commit to pray daily for them for as long as it takes.

- Make plans to deepen a friendship with someone far from God. Do it today. Make a coffee date. Plan to catch a ball game, shoot some pool, scrapbook together, go rock climbing, whatever. No agenda, just face time.

- Look for specific ways to serve the people around you. You care about them, so do something today to prove it.

- Cultivate an awareness of God's work in your life by journaling. Record your prayers—in the future you'll be amazed how he has responded to them. Ask yourself questions like, "What is he teaching me lately?" and record your insights.

F O U R

UNWORTHY

MATTHEW 8:5-13

God gives us direct access to him.

When I was nine years old, I nearly drowned in the ocean.

My grandfather led me out past the breakers to calmer water so we could "really swim." I had won some ribbons on the swim team, and Grandpa wanted to see what I was made of. When he took my hand, I once again admired the tattoo on his arm—just a blue smear by then, barely recognizable as the ship he had etched into his skin during his former days in the U.S. Navy.

"Come on, turkey," he grinned.

He helped me to time the waves, waiting for the right moment as the swell rolled toward us, then hopping and feeling the water lift us up, up, up to the top of the wave. Then we'd float gently down until I could just touch the sand with my toes again. We'd struggle a few more steps, wait, hop, then soar up over another hill of water and glide down again. It was exhilarating, especially when I couldn't touch anymore and had to depend on Grandpa. Grinning mischievously, he squeezed my hand to signal that he would push off and pull me with him up over the swell, when . . .

I went under the water. A rogue wave shoved a wall of water into our faces. When the undertow came rolling back beneath us, it gripped my legs and plucked me out of Grandpa's hand like a gardener pulling a tiny weed. I remember that my cheek was pressed against the sand of the ocean floor. It was very calm, and I was not afraid, thinking, *It will let me go soon.*

In what seemed to me a moment or two later, it did. Then I felt a hand reach under my arm and pull me upwards. I sputtered and tried to gain my bearings as my grandfather dragged me back to shore, looking like he'd seen a ghost. He dropped me on the sand near my mother, sat down, and slowly exhaled.

I was confused and wanted to know why we had turned back. Once he was ready to talk, I found out that the "moment or two" had actually been a minute or two. He dove to find me, searched until he ran out of breath, surfaced for air, and dove again. He didn't know exactly how long I had been under, but I could see that he was rattled.

I sputtered and tried to gain my bearings as my grandfather dragged me back to shore, looking like he'd seen a ghost.

It was a strange experience for me because it wasn't frightening. For whatever reason, the time passed quickly and peacefully for me. Once I understood the danger, though, it certainly did impress upon me a simple imperative: don't mess with the ocean. Or as Grandpa would say, "Respect her."

WHY WOULD HE CARE?

Decades later, I still respect the ocean, and yet, I also can't keep away. Certain things in creation just scream, "Creator!" For you it may be the mountains or the splash of the Milky Way across the night sky away from city lights or the way a fresh snowfall turns your street into a setting fit for a fairy tale. For me, it's the ocean—that mix of unspeakable beauty and untamable power. There's a timelessness in the presence of the ocean, where the water erases any evidence in the sand of our coming and going. The ocean can be so gentle, the sound of the surf as soothing as a mother's song, its waves rocking . . .

There's a timelessness in the presence of the ocean, where the water erases any evidence in the sand of our coming and going.

Just recently, my wife and I took a much-needed vacation to the beaches of South Carolina. I waded out past the breakers and stood gazing over endless waters stretching out farther than the reach of my eyes. The waves came rolling, never ceasing, sometimes lifted me, and set me back down. My breath caught in my throat when, not far off, I saw the curved backs of a pod of dolphins surface and dive in unison, like the coils of a sea serpent. In the midst, literally, of all that power and beauty, I subtly became aware of the presence of the Lord. Some words from Scripture came to mind, an ancient command that he issued to the ocean: "This far you may come and no farther; here is where your proud waves halt" (Job 38:11, *NIV*).

There, rocking in the surging tide, I became aware of the presence of this being who tells the ocean what to do. The ocean could erase me, but God could erase *it*. What an unimaginable God, powerful beyond comprehension. I opened my mouth to pray . . . and then shut it. *Who am I to speak to this God?* I felt, in a word, unworthy.

Perhaps you've also had moments when you glimpsed God's greatness, and appropriately felt small and silly. It may have been a particular sunrise, a moment in corporate worship, the birth of a child, or a truth in Scripture that clicked with you for the first time. The perception can be that God is so far beyond you that he couldn't possibly care what you think. He certainly wouldn't stoop to respond to your needs, would he? How could the God who created the solar system care about whether you make your rent or mortgage payment this month?

Jesus was what God had to say, not in the language
of words, but in the language of humanity.

Feelings like these are based on half of the truth. We *are* unworthy, but that is only part of the story. When we begin to understand God's heart toward our worthiness, it can revolutionize our perspective. He is powerful beyond comprehension, but has made himself approachable. God has revealed a path to wisdom and power that is so widely available, we tend to take it for granted. In a sense, it's a path that is hidden right out in the open—everyone knows about it, but very few people truly use it. If you can have faith to believe it, you can unlock a tremendous source of strength.

There was once an unnamed officer in the Roman army who had that sort of faith, and became one of God's unnamed heroes. Last chapter, we saw how the power of God's message of grace left people astonished. What this man did astonished *God*.

FAITH LIKE THIS

When Jesus was born not too far from the unsuspecting shepherds, "the Word became flesh and made his dwelling among us" (John 1:14, *NIV*). The Word of God became human. Jesus was what God had to say, not in the language of words, but in the language of humanity. If you want to know what God is like, pay attention to Jesus. You can learn a lot about God from his creation and from people's experiences with him. But the best (and the only completely trustworthy) way to learn about God is from the Scripture. And if you desire the clearest vision of God—of what sort of person he is—then read especially the words and deeds of Jesus.

The way Jesus reacted to this unnamed hero says something fascinating about God.

When Jesus returned to Capernaum after preaching the famous Sermon on the Mount, Matthew 8:5 records that an unnamed Roman officer came and pleaded with him. He said, "Lord, my young servant lies in bed, paralyzed and in terrible pain" (v. 6).

Jesus replied simply, "I will come and heal him" (v. 7).

The officer, strangely, turned him down. "Lord, I am not worthy to have you come into my home" (v. 8). This acknowledgment of his own unworthiness showed remarkable sensitivity to Jewish custom, which forbade entering a Gentile's home.[1] The officer's next words revealed an even deeper understanding of who Jesus was. "Just say the word from where you are, and my servant will be healed. I know this because I am under the authority of my superior officers, and I have authority over my soldiers. I only need to say, 'Go,' and they go, or 'Come,' and they come. And if I say to my slaves, 'Do this,' they do it" (vv. 8, 9).

He understood better than many of Jesus' own followers exactly who he was speaking with, and he had the audacity to go for help directly to the one who had all authority.

What a remarkable understanding of Jesus! This man's experience in the military gave him a unique understanding of the nature of authority. A Roman officer commanded considerable control over his soldiers. This officer understood that Jesus commanded that kind of authority over everything. He understood better than many of Jesus' own followers exactly who he was speaking with, and he had the audacity to go for help directly to the one who had all authority. He was neither a theologian nor a philosopher—not one of the religiously brilliant scribes or Pharisees with whom Jesus often debated. He was a professional at violence, a commander of the soldiers who oppressed the Jewish people. Here he was, most likely armed and in armor, not just asking for a miracle from this famous Jewish holy man, but explaining to Jesus how to do it.

"When Jesus heard this, he was astonished" (v. 10, *NIV*). Jesus turned to those who were following him and said, "I tell you the truth, I haven't seen faith like this in all Israel!" (v. 10). Pleasantly surprised by this Gentile's faith, Jesus then used this as an opportunity to explain to his followers that many believers would come from other nations and take their places in the kingdom.

Take note of Jesus' reaction. He did not question, "Who are you to ask such a thing of me, the Son of God?" He did not say, "You're not even one of my followers; what makes you think I would care about your problem?" Instead, Jesus was genuinely impressed with the man's faith and confidence.

He wasn't so bold simply because he didn't understand who Jesus really was. He was bold because he *did*.

"Then Jesus said to the Roman officer, 'Go back home. Because you believed, it has happened.' And the young servant was healed that same hour" (v. 13). I think his reaction says something wonderful about God's willingness to hear from us. Jesus wasn't put off or annoyed with this man's boldness to approach him. Jesus commended him for it.

This Roman soldier had such a steady, confident faith that he went right to the most powerful being in the universe and asked for a miracle. He wasn't so bold simply because he didn't understand who Jesus really was. He was bold because he *did*. His own worthiness or unworthiness was irrelevant, because his faith wasn't in himself but in how capable Jesus was. He understood that he had direct access to the Almighty, and he used it.

DIRECT ACCESS TO GOD

During his days in the military, Colin Powell made it a point to keep communication lines open with his underlings. He wielded so much power that it was often difficult for people to be honest with him.

"In the military, when you become a four-star general, people will do anything you even suggest you want," he explained. "If you say a wall looks a little dirty, by sundown it's painted. You have to be very careful what you say. I had to work at breaking down that deference to hear from my people. All the tables in my office and conference rooms were round so that there was never a head. I would always try not to wear my full uniform. I would always have my jacket and blouse with all the fruit salad on it thrown in the corner."[2]

When you think about what God was willing to do to make it possible for us to relate to him . . . talk about leaving some fruit salad on his jacket! God is so passionate for relationship with us that he became one of us. God became a human baby. Jesus grew, fell down and scraped his knees, and dirtied his feet on the dusty streets. He worked with his hands and sweat under the sun. Jesus came to fulfill a particular mission, to save us, and to remove the guilt that keeps us from him.

It's so common for us to feel like we cannot come directly into God's presence. People want to pray to saints, pray to Mary, or ask some kind of professional to pray for them. Often, we're more likely to ask a pastor to pray about something than we are to pray about it ourselves. If you're thinking that your pastor spends time with God and has been entrusted with spiritual leadership, and so will pray for you if you ask, then great. Ask. When I served on a church staff, I used to love getting requests for prayer—I was honored that people would let me into their hopes and concerns. But if you're thinking that your pastor has some kind of special connection with God that you can't have, you're wrong. Sometimes when people would ask me to pray for something, I'd get this sense that they thought God would be more inclined to do something for them if I asked him to, like I had a direct line or something. I *do* have direct access, but there's nothing special about it at all. You do too. Through Christ, you have direct access to the Almighty.

When Jesus gave up his spirit on the cross, something happened that was full of significance both then and for us today. "At that moment the curtain in the sanctuary of the Temple was torn in two, from top to bottom" (Matthew 27:51). It would be difficult to exaggerate the significance of this. For thousands of years, both in the tabernacle that the Israelites set up in the wilderness and in the permanent temple, an enormous curtain separated the holiest place from the common people. Only the high priest was ever permitted to enter the presence of God in this sacred space, and he was only permitted to do so once a year. Then in one dramatic moment, God ripped the curtain from top to bottom, creating wide-open access to himself.

Your worth does not depend on your worthiness. Acting as if you're not good enough to speak directly with God can be false modesty. This has nothing to do with having confidence in yourself, but in what God did and in the worth he places on you. The Roman officer did not say, "Jesus, I command many men and do a stellar job at it. I try never to kill innocent people, and my family always says grace before supper. Now hear my request." He didn't say anything about himself at all. His confidence was in Jesus.

> Then in one dramatic moment, God ripped the curtain from top to bottom, creating wide-open access to himself.

Hebrews 4:16 says, "So let us come boldly to the throne of our gracious God. There we will receive his mercy, and we will find grace to help us when we need it most." We are all unworthy of God's presence, but Jesus has *made* us worthy. You are worth the blood of Jesus, no less. Do you believe this? If you do, then you could be one of his heroes.

LAST RESORT, OR FIRST RESPONSE?

My training in seminary hadn't prepared me for what happened during worship a few years ago. The band had just started playing, when someone from the back row grabbed my arm and said, "We have to do something!" I followed the path of her pointing finger until my eyes fell upon a woman who was leaning back in her chair as if some unseen force were pushing her over. Her eyes rolled back in her head and her face contorted. I'd never seen anything like it.

Before you get too excited, this wasn't some kind of demonic possession. She was having a massive heart attack. All I knew at the time was that something was seriously wrong. I rushed to the front and grabbed the microphone. The band awkwardly fell silent behind me as I asked, "Is there a doctor in the house?" Now that I know things turned out OK, I can smile about the fact that I actually said those words. "Any nurses, paramedics, firemen . . . please, somebody is very sick." I pointed.

Fortunately, there were many trained emergency professionals at church, and they burst into action. Someone called 911, and the rest of us watched as they went to work. I saw a paramedic and a nurse taking turns administering mouth-to-mouth resuscitation. I saw one of the nurses pounding out chest compressions, and remember thinking to myself, *She's pregnant with twins! She probably shouldn't be exerting herself so much.*

After I don't know how many moments, it occurred to me to lead everyone else in prayer. I'm sure a number of people in the crowd were way ahead of me, but I didn't think to pray until a couple of minutes had passed. We began to pray, and after what felt like a very long time, the woman revived.

One of the paramedics explained to me afterwards that, unlike on television, in real life CPR is often not enough "to bring someone back," especially after so many minutes have passed. When I spoke later with the nurse who had administered the chest compressions, she admitted that she didn't expect the lady to make it, let alone regain consciousness before the ambulance arrived. It cost the poor woman two broken ribs, but she did "come back."

Numerous unnamed heroes leaped into action and saved this woman's life. All I could do was pray. It was sort of my last resort. It seems that's often how it happens—prayer is sort of the last-ditch effort, the thing you do only when there's nothing else you can do. That's certainly how it happens on TV. It's only after the hero has done every conceivable thing he could possibly do that he finally resigns himself with a sigh and says, "All we can do now is pray."

Granted, sometimes action is the name of the game. If someone is having a heart attack, you'd better respond to it. But I suggest that in many situations, prayer ought to be our first inclination instead of our last resort. It's not that we don't have a part to play (we'll talk about that more next chapter). It's that we're not in this alone. You have direct access to the Almighty. We weren't intended to operate according to our own wisdom or by our own strength. We can speak to the one who has authority over all things.

He finally resigns himself with a sigh and says, "All we can do now is pray."

A friend of mine recently got some discouraging news about a ministry she was involved in, a ministry that serves mothers of very young children. Because of the recent economic downturn, their funding had been cut, and they were forced to come up with creative solutions in order to carry on. Some of the cuts were very painful for my friend to accept. For example, every year, this ministry rents a space at a local festival to provide a baby-changing station, complete with free diapers, wipes, hand sanitizer, and some much-needed privacy. It has been a wonderful gift to the community—a very practical expression of God's love. But in the wake of the recent financial depression, there was no money for the fair.

My friend could have tried to meet with church leaders, or tried to raise the money herself. Instead, she prayed. She asked God to take care of it somehow.

The phone rang. It was the coordinator for the fair, wondering if the baby-changing station would be renting a space again this year. When my friend explained why they could not, the coordinator immediately offered to waive the fee.

THINGS THAT ONLY GOD COULD DO

One of Jesus' brothers said, "You don't have what you want because you don't ask God for it. And even when you ask, you don't get it because your motives are all wrong—you want only what will give you pleasure" (James 4:2, 3). It is so simple that we tend to take it for granted. Prayer, simply talking with God, is the pathway to wisdom and power beyond our own. But our motivation is very important. One of the simplest ways to purify your motives is to pray for someone or something other than yourself. Jesus responded to the Roman officer's prayer for his young servant. God responded to my friend's heartfelt prayer that the ministry she was involved in would still be able to serve her community. It's not that God doesn't want us to pray for ourselves—Jesus taught us to pray for our daily bread. It's just that we tend to focus on our own concerns, and God is teaching us to be more like him.

Sometimes, being one of God's heroes is a simple matter of asking God to intervene. Faith-filled, confident, audacious prayers accomplish much. It doesn't depend on us—our worth is never the issue. "Elijah was a man just like us. He prayed earnestly that it would not rain, and it did not rain on the land for three and a half years. Again he prayed, and the heavens gave rain, and the earth produced its crops" (James 5:17, 18, *NIV*). Elijah was a man *just like us*. God has made the most important heroic act—prayer—available to everyone.

Of course, God doesn't always answer our prayers the way we think he should—or according to our timing. His answer is not always yes. Our perspectives are finite, so sometimes we ask for things that appear to be the best thing for us at the time, but ultimately they may not be. Even so, God is not offended by our requests. He wants to hear from us. And when you do pray in accordance with God's will, your words can prompt mountains to jump into the sea.

You don't need to be a name-dropper to make things happen. You don't need friends in high places or access to the wealthy. In Christ, you have direct access to the Almighty. You can speak directly to the one who knows everything, can do anything, and who wants to hear from you.

I was on a short mission trip in Cambodia when this really clicked for me. One of our primary purposes on the trip was to pray for the church-planting ministry that our church supported there. A mentor of mine gave this advice that dramatically changed the way I pray: "Pray often, pray honest, and pray big. Pray for things that only God could do. Pray bigger than you think is reasonable."

Something about that advice struck me and inspired me to change the way I prayed. Looking out of the car window over the miles and miles of Cambodian jungle where thousands of villages of people eke out livings without any Christian presence, I quietly prayed, "Father, would you please plant ten thousand churches in Cambodia?"

You've got direct access to the source of all power and wisdom. You're not talking to a mere human—you're talking to the Almighty. What do you really want to happen?

- Don't just pray that God would bring so-and-so to faith, but that God would eventually use her to bring dozens of other people to faith.
- Don't just pray that God would bring healing with so-and-so's alcoholism, but that God would restore him so completely that he would turn around and help shepherd dozens of other people to wholeness.
- Don't just pray about your bills, anxieties, fears, and concerns. That stuff is important to God, but he knows about it all before you even ask him. Pray that his will would be done through your life.
- Don't limit your prayers to your own dreams, as big as they may seem. God's dreams are bigger. Pray for things that only he can do. Pray that God would do more through you than you can imagine.

Because he can. And that's the theme of the next chapter.

RELEASING **YOUR HEROIC** POTENTIAL

FOR INDIVIDUAL OR GROUP STUDY

1. What sorts of experiences remind you of God's greatness? Nature? Music? Serving? Worship?

2. Have you or someone you know ever experienced a specific response from God to prayer? What happened?

3. Why do you think it's so hard for people to stay faithful in prayer?

4. Regarding your own faithfulness in prayer, what part does your confidence play? What part does your own feeling of worth play?

5. Which is more difficult for you: knowing what to pray, or believing that God will respond? Why?

6. In what ways does prayer change *us*? What about you, specifically? How has speaking with God changed you?

DAILY STEPS TOWARD A HEROIC LIFE

- Pray. If you've gotten off track, then start making some appointments with God again. Carve out ten minutes in the morning, at lunch, or before bed, and take it from there. Be as honest with him as you can be.

- Push your focus out from yourself. Pray for your daily bread, but try to spend more time praising God for who he is, thanking him for what he has done, and praying for his will to be done.

- Develop a discipline of praying for others, or change your discipline if it has grown stale. You could make a list of people for whom you are praying daily. Or dedicate each day of the week to a different group of people (for example, Monday for family, Tuesday for friends, Wednesday for coworkers, Thursday for your church leadership, Friday for a specific missionary in a specific country of the world).

- Push yourself to pray big. In the last chapter, did you commit to pray for some people who are close to you but far from God? Pray huge prayers for them. Slow down and consider God's will for their lives; then pray for it.

FIVE

UNDERESTIMATED

JOHN 6:1-15

God can do more through you than you can imagine.

I spent this last year teaching math to inner-city middle schoolers at a public school in Harlem, New York. Many of my students have some of the same advantages in life that I did growing up—loving parents or incredible caregivers who are doing the best they can. Some of my students hardly stand a chance academically. They live in transitional housing because some man is trying to kill their mother. Or they've suffered terrible abuse themselves. Some of them get to eat only at school. Math just isn't that high on the priority list when you're hungry.

My wife, Lindsay, and I visited friends over Christmas break, and I experienced a moment that caused me to seriously doubt the value of my efforts. When we arrived at our best friends' house, I noticed that they had a giant dry-erase board in the family room. Thinking to myself how much I'd love a dry-erase board like that for my classroom, I asked, "What's this for?" I learned that their daughter was struggling to solve systems of equations—that's multiple equations with multiple variables, for all you non-math-geeks. The girl's father had bought the white board so that they could spend some time working on these sorts of problems together in the evenings.

I felt like someone had hit me in the face with a brick. I thought, *There's no way my kids can compete. I split ninety minutes a day between twenty-five of them, and she gets a private tutor every evening.* In that moment, I saw with clarity how futile my efforts are. At least, that's how it felt.

THE MISSING VARIABLE

I am not suggesting that my friend shouldn't help his daughter because it gives her an unfair advantage over less fortunate kids. That's nonsense. He's a great father, doing exactly the right thing—and I applaud him. In fact, that kind of dedication to a kid's education is pretty rare even among those who have the ability to give it. But it did cause me to question the difference I can really make. My efforts seem a little silly in the face of so many disadvantages.

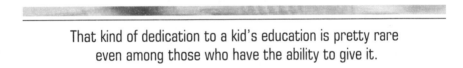

That kind of dedication to a kid's education is pretty rare
even among those who have the ability to give it.

There are many things in life like that. We've all felt it. The problems in the world are so profound that our efforts seem futile. The world is broken. Wars and genocides are like a cancer that can't be beaten. Peace is short-lived—just a remission, really, before the violence flares up again. The issues of poverty are so complicated that few agree even on how to help. Most scientists concur that climate shift is in progress, but there is almost no consensus on its causes or what we can do about it. We're all convinced that how we spend our money matters, but choosing the right priorities can be like trying to catch the wind with a net. Do your purchases support particular nations, fair wages in other countries, and proper treatment of animals—or do you opt for the cheapest items in support of your own family budget?

It is so easy, when you step back and take in the whole picture, to con-clude that you can't really make much of a difference. At one point or an-other, we each ask ourselves a version of this question: *What good is it?* Our efforts for a person, a cause, or an organization are just a drop in the bucket. What's the use in trying?

Honestly, if you're attempting to change the world in your own strength, there may not be much use. But that's like trying to solve a system of equa-tions while ignoring the most important variable. There's something so much bigger and so much more important at work here. We may not be able to change much, but God can change everything.

I'm not sure how well our next unnamed hero understood this. He was, after all, just a boy with very little to offer. If we judge based solely on his actions though, we'd have to say he understood something very important, and no one would have imagined the difference it would make.

WHAT GOOD IS IT?

The boy's story unfolds at the beginning of John 6. It was springtime, and the Sea of Galilee reflected the huge white clouds overhead, rolling across the bright blue sky. Occasionally, the water trembled underneath a cool breeze that swept down from the surrounding mountains. Jesus and his disciples climbed a hill and sat on the grassy slope. They had crossed over to the far side of the sea, hoping to enjoy a moment's respite from the demands of the huge crowd that kept following wherever Jesus went, ex-pecting another miracle (John 6:1-4).

It didn't last. Soon, Jesus saw the crowds approaching, looking for him. He turned to Philip and asked, "Where can we buy bread to feed all these people?" (v. 5). This was one of those rare moments when the text clues us in to Jesus' inner purpose. Verse 6 explains, "He was testing Philip, for he already knew what he was going to do." Jesus' question was a test of Philip's faith. After all the miracles Jesus had performed, how would Philip react?

This was a huge crowd of people. "The men alone numbered about 5,000" (v. 10). Factor in the women and children, and this was perhaps ten to fifteen thousand people, maybe more. Where could they possibly buy bread to feed all these people? Even if there were someplace to get that much food, it would take a small army to move it all. Such a meal required thousands upon thousands of loaves of bread—huge, heaping piles of bread—a grocery store full of bread. The logistics of distributing so much food would make your head hurt. Not to mention the expense. This ragtag bunch of followers maintained a communal purse to use for daily necessities, but otherwise relied heavily on the kindness of strangers. Buying food for so many was simply out of the question.

Maybe Andrew reasoned that something was better than nothing. Or maybe he mentioned it simply to underline how impossible it would be to provide for such a crowd.

Philip sounded a little shocked by Jesus' request. "Even if we worked for months, we wouldn't have enough money to feed them!" (v. 7). Not exactly a huge vote of confidence in Jesus, but who could blame him?

Next, Andrew spoke up, with perhaps a little more faith in Jesus' ability to do *something*. "There's a young boy here with five barley loaves and two fish," he said (v. 9). Maybe Andrew reasoned that something was better than nothing. Or maybe he mentioned it simply to underline how impossible it would be to provide for such a crowd. That's likely the case, because the next thing out of his mouth betrayed his doubt: "But what good is that with this huge crowd?" (v. 9).

And there it is, that sense of futility that we all can fall prey to. "But what good is that . . . ?"

- How far can so little go among so many?
- What difference could it make?
- With so much suffering in the world, what could I possibly do about it?

- Is it really worth trying?

Philip sized up the need and concluded that it would require several months' wages to feed so many. Andrew looked at what they had to offer and concluded that it wasn't enough. It was simple mathematics, and it didn't add up.

But there was one person in this story who acted against better judgment—and proved John Henry Newman's words, that "calculation never made a hero."[1] All we know about that one person is what Andrew said. He was a boy with five barley loaves and two fish, enough food to feed perhaps two or three people. We don't know anything about his appearance, where he came from, or even his name.

How did Andrew know about this boy and his food? Maybe he noticed him earlier and thought to mention it to Jesus after his question. But given Andrew's doubt that it would make any difference, I like to think that this little boy volunteered what he had. I like to think that when Jesus asked Philip how they would feed this huge, approaching crowd, many of his disciples overheard the question. Andrew certainly did. I like to think that this little boy simply and innocently offered to the cause what he had to offer. Perhaps Andrew was even gently patronizing him, highlighting the futility of such a small gesture. It wouldn't be the only time Jesus' followers failed to take children seriously (see Mark 10:13-16). Andrew's question, "But what good is that with this huge crowd?" certainly sounds a little sarcastic.

Whether the boy volunteered what he had or simply offered it willingly when asked, the amazing thing is what happened next.

THEN JESUS

Verse 11 begins with two very powerful words, "Then Jesus." If you read through the New Testament, you'll find that miraculous things often follow those two words. We see someone's small faith, small gesture, or small contribution, and . . . *then Jesus!*

- "*Then Jesus* turned to the paralyzed man and said, 'Stand up, pick up your mat, and go home!'" (Luke 5:24, emphasis added in all these verses).

- "*Then Jesus* rebuked the demon in the boy, and it left him. From that moment the boy was well" (Matthew 17:18).
- "*Then Jesus* said to the woman, 'Your sins are forgiven'" (Luke 7:48).
- "*Then Jesus* placed his hands on the man's eyes again, and his eyes were opened. His sight was completely restored, and he could see everything clearly" (Mark 8:25).
- "*Then Jesus* took her by the hand and said in a loud voice, 'My child, get up!' And at that moment her life returned, and she immediately stood up!" (Luke 8:54, 55).
- "*Then Jesus* shouted, 'Lazarus, come out!'" (John 11:43).
- "*Then Jesus* said to the Roman officer, 'Go back home. Because you believed, it has happened.' And the young servant was healed that same hour" (Matthew 8:13).

On that hillside by the Sea of Galilee, it didn't matter that this boy had only five loaves and two fish for such a huge crowd, because . . . *then Jesus*. John 6:11 says, "Then Jesus took the loaves, gave thanks to God, and distributed them to the people. Afterward he did the same with the fish. And they all ate as much as they wanted." They passed the five loaves of bread and two fish along, each person taking some to eat. Not only did everyone get some, the text is very clear that everyone ate until they were full (vv. 11, 12). When Jesus instructed his disciples to gather all of the leftovers, they filled twelve baskets full of the scraps from the five barley loaves (v. 13).

It's probably safe to say that this boy never dreamed what Jesus could do with his small contribution of fish and bread. If he hadn't volunteered it, Jesus would likely have found another way to feed the crowd, but then our unnamed hero would have missed out on the chance to be involved in such an incredible miracle. If he had held back from contributing because he didn't believe he had enough to make a difference, he never would have had the honor of pointing people to Jesus.

People were physically hungry, and Jesus fed them. God abounds with compassion, and compassion alone is reason enough for any kindness. But that's not the only thing going on here. The people in this crowd ate until they were full, but they would be hungry again. Jesus didn't fix the problem of hunger. Similarly, Jesus brought Lazarus back to life (John 11), but Lazarus died again. At some point after Lazarus stumbled out of that tomb, blinking in the sunlight, he died again. We don't know how many more years he got, but at some point, they ended.

Jesus didn't come to "fix" the world, at least not yet. He said, "You will always have the poor among you" (Matthew 26:11). Don't think for a moment, though, that he means for us to ignore the poor. A quick glance at the Scripture will blast that idea out of the water. Caring for the environment fits hand and glove with God's original purpose for Adam and Eve in the Garden of Eden. Fair wages are just. Followers of the Prince of Peace ought to work for peace on earth. All these things are worth the effort, but we also have to trust that God is working things out. He has promised to set the world right one day—a complete, utter, glorious renewal of all things is coming. In the meantime, we have a crucial part to play in the process of pointing people to Jesus.

On that hillside by the Sea of Galilee, it didn't matter that this boy had only five loaves and two fish for such a huge crowd, because . . . *then Jesus.*

But we may have to get over ourselves a little. God knows what he's doing, and he is working things out for the best. If you offer what you can, I believe you will be amazed one day when he reveals to you all that he accomplished through your life. Like Jesus' followers then, we also tend to ask, "But what good is it?" God's answer is the same today: "Then Jesus." God did more through this unnamed boy's tiny contribution than anyone would have imagined. He can do the same through you. Don't underestimate him.

MORE THAN IMAGINED

My wife is an actress in musical theater. Of course, she always hopes for the "big" parts, but any part is very welcome—a gig is a gig. The saying really is true: "There are no small parts, only small actors." You never know who's watching from the audience—there could be a casting director, an agent, or a reviewer for the *New York Times* out there. You can make an impression with one line, or even with less—a well-timed facial expression can make people laugh or cry. Every character propels the drama. If an actor decides to give something less than 100 percent because he feels his role is too small, the whole show suffers. It can weaken the entire storyline if anybody refuses to take a role seriously.

Unfortunately, that's what some people do with the parts God has given them to play in his story. Say an encouraging word, pray for someone, contribute some money—it sounds either too small to bother, or like it wouldn't be missed if left undone. It can be so tempting to wait for an opportunity to make a "bigger" difference. *Well, if I had a platform like that, of course I'd do something huge for God.* Or, *Sure, if I were a millionaire, I'd contribute all sorts of money to help others.* It's simply not true. If you can't be trusted with little, you won't be trusted with much (see Luke 16:10-12).

> You may not see a tenth of what Jesus does through you on this side of the grave, but be assured, there is a "then Jesus" following your tiny contributions.

Fortunately, there are so many people who do just the opposite. That unnamed boy was certainly not the first nor the last person who would be underestimated. A friend of mine told me about her much older sister-in-law who, in spite of being eighty-one years old, works in an elder care organization taking care of "older people" in their homes! You are not too old, too young, too poor, too powerless, too busy, or too sick to make a difference. Sometimes heroism is found in the smallest gestures. Edgar Watson Howe said, "A boy doesn't have to go to war to be a hero; he can say he doesn't like pie when he sees there isn't enough to go around."[2]

It's so tempting to underestimate the impact that we can have or the difference a particular deed can make. Often when we underestimate ourselves, we actually underestimate God. You never know what Jesus may do—what may follow the "then Jesus"—in response to a tiny act of obedience, generosity, or kindness on your part. God can do more through you than you imagine, so don't ever let the apparent smallness of a gesture give you pause. If God can take a little fish and bread and literally feed thousands, imagine what he could do through a well-timed thank-you note, a phone call to someone who's lonely, or through groceries secretly dropped off on someone's back porch. The story of this unnamed boy can change your attitude about those warmhearted impulses you get to give, serve, encourage, or show kindness. We cannot overestimate what Jesus can do through the smallest heroic act.

A HUNDRED TIMES MORE

In his parable about the different kinds of soil, Jesus said, "Still other seed fell on good soil. It came up and yielded a crop, a hundred times more than was sown" (Luke 8:8, *NIV*). Because Jesus' disciples asked him what this parable meant, this is another of those rare moments in Scripture when we get to glimpse Jesus' deeper meaning.

He explained that the different types of soil represented different types of people and how they respond to the gospel. He said, "The seed on good soil stands for those with a noble and good heart, who hear the word, retain it, and by persevering produce a crop" (v. 15, *NIV*). Hear the word, retain it, and persevere, and you will produce a crop—perhaps even a hundred times what was sown in you. In John 15:5, Jesus reaffirmed, "Yes, I am the vine; you are the branches. Those who remain in me, and I in them, will produce much fruit. For apart from me you can do nothing." Remain in him. Retain the word. Persevere. If you do, you *will* bear much fruit. You may not see a tenth of what Jesus does through you on this side of the grave, but be assured, there is a "then Jesus" following your tiny contributions.

Not too long ago, my friend Leslie came up with a clever way to show her dad some of the impact his example has had on other people. It was his birthday, and she and her brother didn't know what to get him. As usual, he said he didn't want anything. She wanted to do something in honor of her father's lifelong example of kindness and service. That's when she had the great idea to e-mail everyone who knew her father and ask for a favor—not a favor for her dad, but for anybody else. She wrote:

This year we began to think about all the things we have learned from our dad. We both agreed that the greatest thing he has modeled for us is service to others. From bringing sundaes to our elementary school teachers on a hot day, to always feeding the parking meter of his customers, to providing free haircuts to his unemployed or shut-in customers, our father is always giving of himself to others. It is an essential part of his being.

We hope that you will join us in honoring our father's birthday by doing something good for someone else (big or small) in his honor. It can be something as simple as picking up the check for lunch with a friend or as involved as organizing a community cleanup; it's up to you to decide how and whom you will help. We also want this to be fun for you, not a burden—get creative with this! After you have completed your good deed, please e-mail your story to me.

Then she explained that they would print out everyone's responses, have them bound into a book, and present it to her father as a gift for his birthday.

Leslie's e-mail struck a nerve. People were inspired to do all sorts of things in honor of her dad. Many did smaller things—bought breakfast for someone, helped out with an event at church, paid the toll for the cars behind them at the tollbooth.

Some did bigger things. For example, one teacher, after finally receiving the fish she had ordered, spent a lot of time and energy setting up the aquarium she had long desired for her classroom. But then she decided to deliver it to *another* teacher's classroom in honor of Leslie's dad. The experience was so rewarding for her that she decided to repeat it—she set up aquariums as gifts for more teachers' rooms.

Some people served others in such a way that it prompted them to "pay it forward." One lady who manages the scholarship program for lower-income families at a local fitness club began offering lower rates to families, with the agreement that when they were able to, they would then turn around and pass along the blessing to others. The families loved it. One dad in particular got a pay raise and began paying the full membership fee and some extra each month in order to beef up the scholarship fund so other families could benefit from it.

**Some people served others in such a way
that it prompted them to "pay it forward."**

It must have been a wonderful moment when Leslie's dad read through the e-mails describing all the kind and generous things people had done to honor his example. Our tiny little offerings may just be a drop in the bucket—a drop in an ocean of need. One drop won't change the ocean, but consider the ripple effect! My friend's dad got a tiny glimpse of just how far the ripples reached.

WHAT GOOD IT *IS*

When I think about my students, I know some of them won't be able to compete in the world of mathematics. Some of them will. For some of them, the challenges they've had to overcome will make them even more successful. For the rest, I have decided not to underestimate Jesus.

One day last year, I decided to teach all my students how to shake hands. (I got the idea from a fellow teacher. Thanks, Theresa!) All of my students had to shake my hand before they could come into class. They had to do it right. "Make solid contact here. No squid fingers . . . connect! No, a firm grip, but don't squeeze. OK, good. Now look me in the eye. Perfect." Once they got it right, I said something like, "There you go. That's how you're going to land that job," or, "That's how you're going to open a savings account," or, "That's how you'll seal the deal." Just a drop in the bucket, really. Just a few loaves of bread and a couple fish.

Imagining the "then Jesus" part makes me smile though. Maybe this student will make the right impression at a college interview. Maybe that one will get a business loan. Maybe she will have a little more confidence to face her difficult life head-on. Maybe he will make a good impression with his future father-in-law. You never know what might follow when Jesus gets involved. There could be baskets full of leftovers.

Don't doubt your contribution, and don't underestimate Jesus. Of course, if you do doubt, there's some good news about that too, as you'll discover in the next chapter. For now though, simply recognize God's ability to do more through you than you can imagine. "Now to him who is able to do immeasurably more than all we ask or imagine, according to his power that is at work within us, to him be glory in the church and in Christ Jesus throughout all generations, for ever and ever! Amen" (Ephesians 3:20, 21, *NIV*).

RELEASING **YOUR HEROIC** POTENTIAL

FOR INDIVIDUAL OR GROUP STUDY

1. If you could wave a magic wand and fix one problem in the world, what would you fix? Why?

2. Think of something small that someone did for you or said to you that had a huge impact on your life. What is it, and why did it mean so much to you? Was there a "then Jesus" moment connected with this experience? What was it?

3. Which statement do you think is a more dangerous outlook: a) "This world is all that matters, so we need to fix it," or b) "God is going to destroy this world, so it's not worth trying to change things"? Why?

4. How does the story of the unnamed slave girl and Naaman's conversion in chapter 1 illustrate the ripple effect described in this chapter?

5. What's a small thing you could do this week for:

- Your spouse?

- Your children?

- A friend?

- Your parents?

- Your boss?

- A neighbor?

- Your church?

DAILY STEPS TOWARD A HEROIC LIFE

- Write a thank-you note or thank someone in person for something small he or she did that meant a lot to you.

- Follow my friend Leslie's example and use her gift idea for someone in your life who has set an example of kindness and service.

- Use your resources to contribute toward things with eternal significance. You may not see the difference it makes now, but one day you will be glad for every penny you spend selflessly.

- If you are not involved in serving regularly, then it's time to get in the game. The little things we do matter—don't underestimate them—and they can make a huge difference when God works through them. Nothing is better than having been used by God.

SIX

UNCERTAIN

MARK 9:14-27

God desperately wants to help us believe.

W e have looked at how God makes heroes out of people we might least expect. Neither our brokenness nor our sin can prevent God from using us to accomplish his will. He works through untrained people—we don't need special skills to serve him. The unnamed heroes in the last two chapters demonstrated some very encouraging principles—truth so vital that living it can mean the difference between a heroic life and a wasted life. You have direct access to God, and he can do more through you than you can imagine.

The question is, do you believe it?

A FAITHLESS PEOPLE

There are so many reasons *not* to believe. Life can certainly test your certainty. If you aren't in the crucible now, you likely will be at some point. I don't want to be pessimistic, just truthful. Life is periodically hard, and it will attempt to break your resolve to trust God. No one is immune from it—even the most fortunate among us will face some struggle to believe. When things spin out of your control, that's when you find out whether you really believe that God is in control.

The most severe tests of faith often come when something terrible happens to someone we love. In my estimation, parents face some of the greatest tests of faith. Even in the best circumstances, it requires a heaping dose of trust to watch your little one walk to school on his own for the first time. The ride home from moving him into his first college dorm room isn't any easier. In the worst cases, parents helplessly wring their hands as their children join gangs, shoot up, or make themselves throw up. I can't imagine a bigger test to having faith in a loving, benevolent God than through losing a loved one—especially a child.

When my childhood best friend died a few years ago (in a mysterious scuba diving accident from which they never recovered his body), there was nothing I could say to his mother about God's plan. It wasn't appropriate to say anything trite about having faith or about God working things out for the best. I missed my friend terribly, and my own certainty in God's presence and purposes was worn pretty thin. All I could offer was, "God understands. He understands what it's like to lose a son."

> When things spin out of your control, that's when you find out whether you really believe that God is in control.

Tests come in various forms and levels of intensity. Some are very minor—for example, when somebody snubs you and you must decide if your love is the sort that "keeps no record of being wronged" (1 Corinthians 13:5). Some tests are much more severe. Most of us would affirm that God will provide for us, but it's when you get let go from your job that your faith comes under fire. You (or someone you know) may feel trapped in a marriage that seems damaged beyond repair, and any faith you have in God's ability to restore has taken a series of punches to the gut. You may be very ill, or caring for someone who is very ill, and your unanswered prayers may be shaking your confidence that God can or will do anything about it.

Seemingly unanswered prayer can pose some of the worst wounds to faith. In fact, it can kill faith. If you've got unresolved issues regarding unanswered prayer, I suspect it's been a real struggle to take this book seriously after chapter 4 about the Roman officer. *Pray big . . . sure, I'll get right on that.* I know people who gave up walking with God when what seemed like a very reasonable prayer—a prayer that you'd think a good God would want to answer—just wasn't answered. She died. He failed. It flopped. And there was silence from Heaven.

Our faith is solid after periods of spiritual depth when we see reasons to believe, but when life pulls the rug out from under us, our certainty falters.

When you face a test to your faith, you might be caught in a tension between certainty and doubt. We do believe, but we also doubt. Some people have a naturally strong faith and are able to help others to believe. In fact, faith is one of the gifts of the Spirit (1 Corinthians 12:9). Others struggle to believe. Their relationships with God can often feel like wandering in the dark with their hands outstretched, hoping they'll bump into something real.

Most of us go through ups and downs. Our faith is solid after periods of spiritual depth when we see reasons to believe, but when life pulls the rug out from under us, our certainty falters.

Yet the Bible says, "Without faith it is impossible to please God, because anyone who comes to him must believe that he exists and that he rewards those who earnestly seek him" (Hebrews 11:6, *NIV*). Does that mean that when we doubt we cannot please God? After all, "faith is being sure of what we hope for and certain of what we do not see" (v. 1, *NIV*). Faith is being *certain* of what we do not see. Where does that leave all of us who occasionally struggle with uncertainty?

God doesn't want us to be in the dark about this, and he understands fully the stress that everyday life can put on faith. Faith *is* being sure of what we hope for and certain of what we do not see, but that doesn't say anything about where faith comes from. A look at our next unnamed hero can help.

There's a story in Scripture about an unnamed father who helplessly watched his son suffer for years. His faith had been tested to the limit, and his heart was a battleground between certainty and doubt. The way this man approached Jesus—just as he was, struggling to believe—provides a powerful example of faith in the midst of uncertainty. This man didn't have certainty; but as far as Jesus was concerned, what he did have was enough.

A FATHER'S STRUGGLING FAITH

This father's story comes at an interesting moment in Jesus' ministry. In Mark 9:2-13, Jesus had taken Peter, James, and John to a mountaintop and transformed before their eyes into the dazzling radiance of his heavenly body. Elijah and Moses, both long dead, appeared and spoke with him. The three disciples were frightened and awed, and unsure of how to react. Finally, the Father spoke from a cloud, his powerful voice rumbling. It was an intense spiritual experience.

Our story begins as they descended from the mountain to find a large crowd rallied around the other disciples, who were arguing with some teachers of religious law (v. 14). They came down from hearing the voice of the Father in a cloud to this theological street fight. Isn't that always the way of it? Oftentimes an intense spiritual experience is followed by a disappointing fall back into everyday life. A powerful worship service, a life-altering conference, a visible answer to prayer, a loved one giving his life to Christ, and then . . . diapers still need to be changed, your boss is still riding you about that presentation, the trash needs to be taken out, that English paper isn't going to just write itself.

When the crowd saw Jesus, they ran to greet him, but he asked, "What is all this arguing about?" (v. 16). I imagine an awkward moment or two. If men had worn hats in those days, I think they'd have nervously twisted them in their hands. Many of the things we argue about are important, but I wonder how we'd explain some of our debates if Jesus stepped into the room and asked us that question.

Many of the things we argue about are important, but I wonder how we'd explain some of our debates if Jesus stepped into the room.

After who-knows-how-many moments of sidelong glances and wondering who would try to defend his position first, a man from the crowd spoke up. "Teacher, I brought my son so you could heal him. He is possessed by an evil spirit that won't let him talk. And whenever this spirit seizes him, it throws him violently to the ground. Then he foams at the mouth and grinds his teeth and becomes rigid. So I asked your disciples to cast out the evil spirit, but they couldn't do it" (vv. 17, 18). Listen to the frustration and disappointment in this father's voice. "I brought my son so *you* could heal him," he said, "but *they* couldn't do it."

Jesus replied, "You faithless people! How long must I be with you? How long must I put up with you?" (v. 19). Jesus sounds frustrated, but notice that he wasn't specifically frustrated with this unnamed father. "You faithless *people!*" he said.

But then he added, "Bring the boy to me."

The evil spirit threw the boy to the ground and into violent convulsions. He writhed on the ground, foaming at the mouth. This was obviously a serious case. Jesus asked the boy's father, "How long has this been happening?" (vv. 20, 21).

In the father's reply you hear the anguish of a parent who has watched his son suffer for years: "Since he was a little boy. The spirit often throws him into the fire or into water, trying to kill him" (vv. 21, 22). Then, hoping that Jesus might possibly be able to do something where his disciples had failed, he pleaded, "Have mercy on us and help us, if you can."

This unnamed father's shaky faith was enough.

Jesus' response was pointed. He asked, "What do you mean, 'If I can'?" Then he explained, "Anything is possible if a person believes" (v. 23).

Then this unnamed father gave words to the heart's cry of so many believers when he exclaimed, "I do believe, but help me overcome my unbelief!" (v. 24). He wanted to believe, but he was unsure. He was willing, but uncertain—just as so many of us are today.

Jesus commanded the spirit to leave and never to return. Then the spirit, like an angry kid throwing a temper tantrum, threw the boy into one last convulsion before departing, leaving his body as lifeless as a corpse. People even murmured that the boy was dead, and I imagine that his father hung his head in despair. "But Jesus took [the boy] by the hand and helped him to his feet, and he stood up" (vv. 25-27).

This unnamed father's shaky faith was enough. He wasn't 100 percent certain, but he was willing to believe. His desire to believe and willingness to ask for help outweighed his unbelief. His simple prayer to Jesus illustrates a vital truth about faith. Jesus did not say to this father, "You know what, come back when you're 100 percent sure!" Instead, Jesus responded to his request, and helped him to believe. Jesus' posture is the same toward us today. God wants to help us believe.

THE FAITHFUL FATHER

God is patient with uncertainty, and the Bible says that we should be too.

Jude 22 says, "Be merciful to those who doubt" (*NIV*). When Thomas told the other disciples he would need to actually stick his finger in Jesus' nail wounds before he would believe that his Lord really had come back from the grave, he earned himself a nickname that has stuck to him for almost two thousand years. But Jesus never called him Doubting Thomas. He simply said, "Put your finger here; see my hands. Reach out your hand and put it into my side. Stop doubting and believe" (John 20:27, *NIV*). It's not that doubting is unimportant. Doubt is spiritually dangerous and emotionally painful—and salvation comes by faith. But God does understand the challenges we face to believe. He may grow frustrated, wishing we could enjoy the peace of mind that comes from a firm faith, but he is patient with us.

> This unnamed father's appeal to Jesus voices our own
> inner tension, but also the path to resolution.

What we believe is critical. Faith involves our minds. "Faith comes from hearing the message" (Romans 10:17, *NIV*). Some people are utterly convinced of the wrong things, and the consequences can be terrifying. But there is more to faith than *what* we believe. It also involves our hearts—the center of ourselves, the seat of our wills, our capacity to choose. It is in our hearts that we must choose to believe, and the feelings of certainty can follow. "For it is with your heart that you believe" (v. 10, *NIV*).

This unnamed father's appeal to Jesus voices our own inner tension, but also the path to resolution. He cried, "I do believe, but help me overcome my unbelief!" He wanted to believe, chose to believe, and asked God's help for his uncertainty. Notice the role that he played in his own faith and the role that God played. He chose, God helped. An important step in a growing faith is to make this choice to ask for help, over and over, in as many circumstances as call for it. This man's prayer gives us a model of how to relate to God in the midst of doubt or uncertainty. I've used his exact words before: "Father, I do believe, but help me with my unbelief!"

In the situations you face, you may need to pray:

- "God, I believe that you can help my marriage, but I'm having a hard time believing that you will. Help me believe!"
- "Lord, I do believe that you will provide for us, but I can't see any way that this could possibly work out. Help me to trust you."
- "Father, I can't survive this—it's just too much. And I'm beginning to doubt very seriously that you care. I want to trust you, but I don't."

If you can pray this way—if you can invite God into your uncertainty and let him meet you in your doubt, then you've taken a huge step toward faith. The opposite approach involves trying to fake it or cover up the fact that you are unsure—but God sees through that anyway. He takes prayers seriously if you're honest and really mean them.

I found this out firsthand before I had any faith at all. Years ago, I was an atheist. One day I said out loud to an empty room, "OK, 'god,' if you really do exist and you really are all powerful, then you could make me believe in you. So if that's the case, then why don't you just make me believe? Give me faith." It didn't occur to me then that I was actually praying . . . and I had no idea what I was getting myself into!

Praying this way isn't a magic formula to get things to go your way. It is simply a way to relate to God when you doubt him. Maybe you'll be like the unnamed father whose son was healed, or maybe you'll be like the disciples who failed to cast the spirit out. Choosing to trust God won't take away all the failure, struggle, and pain. Sometimes failure comes be-cause of doubt. Later, after Jesus cast the spirit out, his disciples asked him privately why they couldn't cast it out. He explained that it was because of a lack of prayer. He didn't offer them a formula prayer for exorcism; he only explained that they needed to pray—that they needed a closer walk with God.

On the other hand, the fact that you're going through something pain-ful doesn't necessarily mean you're lacking something or doing something wrong. Often life is just hard. Sometimes we suffer for doing the *right* thing. During those times, we must try to realize the same thing I said to my friend's mom: "God understands." If you are living in that place now, I encourage you to take it one day at a time, one prayer at a time, and ask for his help to believe that he is with you, that he is good, and that he loves you.

CERTAIN ENOUGH

Often, choosing to believe naturally expresses itself in action, which is an important part of faith. Faith involves our minds and our hearts, but also our actions. The book of James says, "Faith by itself, if it is not accompanied by action, is dead" (2:17, *NIV*). Our actions can never earn God's acceptance—we can only be right with God by accepting the free gift of his grace, and we can only accept that gift through faith. But our actions show what sort of faith we have (v. 18). When we find something outrageously funny, we spontaneously laugh—our actions spring forth from our beliefs. And our actions complete our faith (v. 22). Choosing to act in accordance with our beliefs confirms and strengthens our faith. A growing faith is a dance between our hearts and minds, our actions and experiences, and the help of our God.

A growing faith is a dance between our hearts and minds, our actions and experiences, and the help of our God.

It's one thing to understand in your mind that a chair is properly built, the loads calculated accurately, and to believe it will support your weight. It's another thing altogether to go and sit on the chair. That's faith expressing itself in action. It's one thing to understand the Scriptures that say God will provide for you. It's another thing altogether to tithe. I don't know anyone who has made the decision to begin to give intentionally and regularly who hasn't experienced a corresponding reduction in anxiety about money. It's not that you give in order to get something—blessings or inner peace about money. You give out of love and obedience to the Lord, and the strengthened faith is a wonderful side effect.

Often, we have a part to play in God's response to our prayers. We will have to apologize or ask for help or seek counseling. Do you *really* believe? Then you've got to actually sit on the chair.

It's not wrong to want to be certain about something, but don't allow yourself to be paralyzed while waiting for 100 percent certainty. Faith is being certain of what we do *not* see. A huge spiritual lightbulb lit up for my younger brother when he realized the futility of reaching complete certainty, and then he decided to give his life to Christ. He was carpooling with some buddies on the way to work, and they were talking about girls. One of the guys wanted to ask a young lady out, and was trying to work up the courage to do so. Another guy admitted, "I could never ask a girl out unless I was 100 percent certain that she would say yes." When my brother heard that, he thought, *But you can never be 100 percent certain that anyone will say yes.* He realized that if he lived according to his friend's mind-set, he would never ask any girl out, ever.

In that moment, all the months of reading the Bible, weighing evidence, and considering Christ became crystal clear. He decided to trust Christ. He wasn't completely certain, but he was certain enough.

100 PERCENT WILLING

The deeds prompted by people who were "certain enough" are just plain inspiring. When I started digging into the stories of unnamed heroes, I was so encouraged by the things Christians are doing in the world. Historically, people have done some pretty terrible things in the name of Christ, often earning the church a bad reputation. At the other extreme, people have also made incredible contributions to society over the centuries. But I am most impressed by the everyday heroes—the regular believers who dig down into their sometimes shaky faith to do something heroic. You don't hear a lot about them, because they aren't always glamorous or "newsworthy," but I think their untold stories represent the true story of the church.

Just as losing a child is one of the greatest tests to faith, caring for a child in need is one of faith's greatest expressions. James said this: "Pure and genuine religion in the sight of God the Father means caring for orphans and widows in their distress and refusing to let the world corrupt you" (James 1:27). The faith of these ordinary heroes is certainly expressing itself in these types of works.

My friend Justin in Cincinnati told me about an executive at a large company there who completely changed a young boy's future. This woman heard about the boy from a coworker who coaches the company Little League baseball team. According to the coach, one of the boys on the team had huge potential, but little opportunity. His mother was single and money was very tight. The executive went to one of the games and approached the boy and his mother with a surprising offer. She told him that if he would get all A's in school, she would pay for his college. The kid's B+ average jumped to an A average in no time.

Jenny and Danielle told me about an elementary school teacher who actually chose to *become* a single mom so that she could provide a home for children who didn't have one. Teaching so many children who didn't have a stable home to return to at the end of the school day prompted her to consider adoption. Over time, she realized it was a calling. She flipped her entire life and schedule upside down and adopted two sisters who needed a home. Sometime later, she adopted a third little girl. My friend Danielle recalled, "When I saw her with this new little girl, I could just see the peace of Christ washed over her. It was evident to me that she is fulfilling God's purpose for her life as she continues to walk out in faith!"

The kid's B+ average jumped to an A average in no time.

Yet another friend, Tabitha, reminded me of a couple who were just on the verge of becoming empty nesters, when everything changed. They were really looking forward to the free time they hadn't enjoyed in decades, but it was becoming clear that their daughter was not able to care for their granddaughter. So they took a deep breath and decided to raise the child. The peace and quiet they were supposed to have is now filled up with parent-teacher conferences, father-daughter events, and a houseful of neighborhood kids wanting to play. Their hair may be turning gray a bit faster, but I'm sure their hearts will stay young longer.

I wish I had the space to tell you about the couple Wendy knows, who raised their own four sons, and then began to foster babies, and then adopted two sisters, and then adopted another little girl, and then adopted four siblings with various special needs—who are now the parents of ten former orphans!

I wish I had the space to tell you about Becky's parents, who after raising their own children, forsook the empty nest and began to adopt. Their example inspired one of their own daughters to adopt as well.

Regardless of whatever reputation the church may have in the headlines at a particular time, I can tell you this: God's unnamed heroes are doing the work of Jesus all over the world.

Reading so many stories about how Christian people are caring for orphaned children has been one of the most encouraging, faith-affirming experiences of my life.

I had the privilege of visiting an amazing family in Kherson, Ukraine. My friend Rob recently reminded me about them—how desperate the situation in their country was, and how this couple responded. Following the collapse of the Soviet Union, economic hardships led many people who could not or would not care for their children to abandon them to the streets. Eventually there was a huge population of homeless children. As you can imagine, these kids did whatever they could to survive—prostitution, for one—and didn't usually survive long. Not so for at least twelve of them though. That's how many this couple in Ukraine adopted. They took them in, fed them, taught them, raised them, and loved them. With very modest means, they saved twelve lives. Literally. When we visited, the kids played the violin and sang for us. The older ones practiced their English. The tiny ones darted around and smiled up at us like little elves. You should have seen the smiles on their faces—the genuine, natural smiles of kids who are loved.

Regardless of whatever reputation the church may have in the headlines at a particular time, I can tell you this: God's unnamed heroes are doing the work of Jesus all over the world. Quietly, behind the scenes, followers of Jesus feed, clothe, and shelter the poor; provide clean water; build orphanages, hospitals, and schools . . . The efforts of God's unnamed heroes are changing everything, and God wants you to be one of them.

This world is a dark place that tests your faith. The fact that there are children out there who resort to prostitution for survival can rattle your belief in a good God. The fact that there's a demand for their business can wreck any positive view of humanity. But when you look at what people do in response to faith in Christ—real, everyday, unnamed believers—it's as if the clouds part and the light of God breaks through. In faith, God's people provide, heal, teach, build, adopt, and love. In the midst of a world of doubt and confusion, they believe—and act on their beliefs. They are the salt that subtly changes the flavor of the entire world. They are the lights in the darkness.

Are you one of them?

RELEASING YOUR HEROIC POTENTIAL

FOR INDIVIDUAL OR GROUP STUDY

1. Do you think it is possible to believe in Christ but not act any differently? Conversely, do you think it's possible to "act like a Christian" but not believe? How have you seen this evidenced in someone's life? What do you think is the right relationship between faith and action?

2. Can you remember a time when your faith was tested? What happened? How did you pull through? What lessons did you learn?

3. Do you think belief is more an individual or corporate thing? What role does the individual play in faith? What role does the community or fellowship of believers play in faith?

4. How would you describe your faith right now? Choose all that apply, and be honest.

_____ "I believe."

_____ "I'm trying to believe."

_____ "I'm struggling to believe."

_____ "I'm not sure I buy all of this."

_____ "I used to believe, but something happened."

Explain your response.

5. What is difficult and challenging in your life right now? What do you believe about God's involvement in regard to this difficulty? Is there anything you need to do in response to your faith?

DAILY STEPS TOWARD A HEROIC LIFE

- Spend some time talking to God about your faith, right now. First, be perfectly honest with him. Next, talk to him about it. If your faith is strong, thank him. If you are struggling with uncertainty, ask for his help.

- Take some time to journal about your faith. Identify the things about God that you struggle to fully accept. Do you have a hard time believing in who Jesus was? in God's forgiveness? in his willingness to help? that he has a plan for you? Something else?

- When you pray, practice thanking God for the things he has done in your life, or proven about himself. Thank him for times he provided for you, healed you, comforted you. Remembering what he has done will strengthen your faith for the present.

- If there is something you need to *do* to live out your faith—some action you need to take in order to complete your inner belief—then do it. In faith, take the first step today.

SEVEN

UNNOTICED

MARK 12:41-44

God sees the heart.

I want to let you in on a joke that my wife and I share. Every time we see a tip jar in a restaurant, she gives me a mischievous grin. If she really wants to drive me up a wall, she'll pluck a dollar out of her purse and slowly, deliberately, dramatically place it into the jar. She does this because she knows it drives me crazy. I dislike the attention.

It started with a *Seinfeld* episode. The character George Costanza had an issue at a restaurant where he bought calzones. He explained to Jerry that just as he went to put a dollar in the tip jar, the worker in the restaurant looked the other way and missed it. When the worker turned back, he gave George a look that seemed to say, "Thanks for nothing." George summarized the experience by asking, "I mean, if they don't notice it what's the point?"

Jerry responded, "So you don't make it a habit of giving to the blind."

"Not bills," George replied.

Then of course, this became a subplot for the rest of the episode. Later, in an attempt to be noticed, George made a dramatic show of placing a dollar in the tip jar, but once again, the worker looked the other way at exactly the wrong moment. Refusing to let his tip go unnoticed, George reached into the jar to retrieve it, so that he could put it back in when the worker was watching.

The worker turned back just in time to see George taking the dollar *out* of the tip jar. That got the worker's attention all right. It also got George banned from his favorite calzone place.[1]

GETTING ATTENTION

When I leave a tip, it's out of appreciation for good service, not to be noticed. I'd much rather hide it under a glass on the table and get out before it's collected. I don't like that kind of attention, and my wife knows it, which is why she has a little fun at my expense with the tip jar.

But before you think my motives are always pure, I must admit that there are other areas in life in which I do crave recognition. I definitely want some of the things I do to be noticed. For whatever reason, this is especially true when it comes to doing chores around the house. I don't know how many times I've made my wife roll her eyes when, fishing for some recognition, I said something like, "There sure were a lot a dirty dishes earlier." Meanwhile, she was probably thinking, *What do you want, a cookie? I did the dishes the last three days!*

What can I say? I need a lot of encouragement.

It's natural for us to crave recognition. It can be painful when you stay up all hours of the night to meet a deadline, but never hear "thanks" from the boss. Or if someone else takes the credit for your good idea, it can just burn you up. Students who work hard on a paper expect to see some kind of indication that their instructor actually read it—a check mark here and there, preferably a comment or two. And while the vast majority of the work of parents and caregivers goes unnoticed, hopefully there's at least a card on the appropriate holiday.

It's natural for us to crave recognition. It can be painful when you stay up all hours of the night to meet a deadline, but never hear "thanks" from the boss.

When hard work goes unnoticed, it can cause real problems. Many marriages sour simply because everyday contributions to the team are taken for granted. Employees stop "going above and beyond the call of duty," and instead skate by with the bare minimum. Everyday deeds can begin to be labeled as drudgery rather than a gift given. Worse, you can begin to lose your drive to do the right thing, or in some cases even to serve God and the people around you.

Encouraging and thanking one another is very important. The Bible instructs us to honor and to encourage one another (Romans 12:10; 1 Thessalonians 5:11). What about all the dozens of things we do that go unnoticed? None of us can control our boss, spouse, kids, or anybody else. So how do we go unnoticed day in and day out and maintain our drive and joy in serving?

The answer is a little surprising: we *don't* go unnoticed.

GETTING GOD'S ATTENTION

Jesus does not look at things in the same way that we do. Our next unnamed hero did something that seemed so insignificant that none of us would have noticed. As you read her story from Mark 12:41-44, pay attention to what got Jesus' attention.

There are some surprising things about this passage. For starters, Jesus went into the temple and chose a seat where he could watch the crowds drop their money into the collection box. Apparently, Jesus either didn't know or didn't care that we modern-day Americans would consider that to be impolite. It's inappropriate for us to ask people about how much they make or how much their homes cost. Sitting and watching how much people plunked down in the offering box would be just plain rude in our culture. But that's exactly what Jesus did.

He watched as "many rich people put in large amounts" (Mark 12:41), and he didn't say a thing. That seems a little surprising, both then and now. I can't help but notice the big contributions. In the church I am currently a part of, someone once dropped $20,000 in the offering plate when he learned of a budget shortfall. This person had $20,000 . . . *in cash* . . . *on him*! I admit, I took note.

We notice when the very wealthy found orphanages, establish scholarship funds, and build community centers. All of that is great stuff, but here Jesus watched the very large contributions of the rich—and remained silent.

Then a widow approached the collection box—not just any widow, a *poor* widow. Into the box she placed "two small coins." These were two very small coins that in Greek were called *lepta*, and were worth "only a fraction of a penny" (v. 42, *NIV*).

Pennies today are almost worthless. In fact, to our government, they are less than worthless—they may be *costing* money. The *New York Times* reported: "In the latest only-in-Washington episode, we find that the government may have lost as much as $40 million coining pennies and nickels last year."[2] The metal in the coins cost more than the coins are worth. It's hard to think of something less significant than a penny. We leave them in cups at the convenience store counter to share with others. If the bill comes up to something.99, I say to the clerk, "Don't worry about the penny"—it's not worth it to me to carry it in my pocket. Often when I owe a penny, the clerk will waive it. If I drop a penny, it's usually not worth my effort to bend over and pick it up. And while I do have one friend who's cheap enough to dodge traffic for a found penny, he's at least got the sense to laugh at himself for it (love ya, Dad!).

This very poor widow came and dropped just part of a penny into the box—not even an entire penny, but just a fraction of one.

The text says that Jesus "called his disciples to him" (v. 43). Jesus gathered his disciples around because he had something significant to say. No one would have noticed this woman or her insignificant contribution, but Jesus did, and he called his followers over to explain why it was important. "I tell you the truth, this poor widow has given more than all the others who are making contributions," Jesus said (v. 43).

I imagine his disciples interrupted with the first-century equivalent of "Say what?"

I imagine his disciples interrupted with the first-century equivalent of "Say what?"

Jesus explained, "For they gave a tiny part of their surplus, but she, poor as she is, has given everything she had to live on" (v. 44).

Jesus noticed what no one else could. The large contributions of the rich were only tiny fractions of their abundance. The fraction of a penny from this unnamed widow was actually all she had to live on. Sometimes the things that go completely unnoticed by the world get God's attention.

GOD SEES THE HEART

About a thousand years before this, Samuel learned a valuable lesson about how God views the world. King Saul had become corrupt, and so the Lord sent Samuel to the household of Jesse in order to anoint a replacement. One of Jesse's sons was to become the new king.

When Samuel saw Jesse's son Eliab, he thought to himself, "Surely the LORD's anointed stands here before the LORD" (1 Samuel 16:6, *NIV*). But the Lord said to him, "Do not consider his appearance or his height, for I have rejected him. The LORD does not look at the things man looks at. Man looks at the outward appearance, but the LORD looks at the heart" (v. 7, *NIV*).

He's not after your time, energy, or resources—
he longs for the complete devotion of your heart.

I believe that is what Jesus noticed about this woman's sacrifice: he noticed her heart. She was a poor widow, obviously living day-to-day. This was perhaps the little bit of money that was left from begging or from the kindness of neighbors, after she had eaten that day. Instead of keeping it, she demonstrated a radical trust in God's provision by giving it up. The faith and trust in this woman's heart far exceeded that of the other contributors.

A friend of mine named Andrew witnessed similar sacrifices when he lived in Ukraine. It came time for the church there to build a new building. People did not have much money, so they began to sell things to buy materials for the building. They sold jewelry; some people sold their wedding rings. People sold furniture and rugs from their homes.

Andrew explained, "Unlike our lifestyle, where we might welcome the chance to give away old furniture so we could buy new, for some of these people, there would be no realistic prospect of ever replacing what was given up."

Usually, when I donate clothes or a piece of furniture, it's to get rid of it or make room for more—it's just a tiny fraction out of my surplus. When these people in the Ukraine donated, it was a real sacrifice, and God saw their hearts.

Andrew also witnessed Americans making similar sacrifices. One woman retrieved her wedding dress out of her hope chest and sent it along to a clothing ministry in Ukraine so that someone else could use it. God is pleased with the heart behind such gestures.

God sees the heart. I can't think of a message that is so simultaneously challenging and freeing. On the one hand, it completely levels the playing field. God isn't watching to see how much you have—whether time, energy, or resources—but what you do and are willing to do with what you have. On the other hand, God wants a whole lot more than our stuff. He wants our hearts. He won't be bribed or bargained with. He won't settle for less. He's not after your time, energy, or resources—he longs for the complete devotion of your heart.

Let me explain. Last chapter, we talked about actually "sitting on the chair"—how faith isn't a living faith if it is not expressing itself in action. The illustration I gave had to do with regular, intentional giving, so let's stick with that (though we could just as easily talk about your time, energy, skills, etc.). God wants us to practice the discipline of generosity because he longs for our hearts, not for our money. If you are tithing regularly in order to appease God so that you can do whatever you wish with the rest of your money, then you are operating out of a spiritually dangerous confusion. If giving is for you just another bill to pay, or worse, if you're just trying to get God off your back, then it would be better for you to keep your money.

A heart fully devoted to God holds all things with an open hand. For the heart devoted to God, regular tithing is an important expression of faith, obedience, and trust. A real expression of trust might mean giving more sacrificially. If we aren't going without something in order to give, are we really giving? Plus, real giving is much more challenging than just picking an amount. It's actually about the attitude of your heart. Only you know whether your generosity is an expression of a heart fully devoted to God. Jesus spoke about money so often because he understood that our hearts would go wherever our money goes (Matthew 6:21). Jesus wanted our hearts to be in the right place.

This applies to all areas of your life. If you go to church on Sundays or spend an hour a day in prayer so that you can forget about God for the rest of the week, then where is your heart? If you volunteer your talents at church so you won't feel guilty about bending your integrity at work, then where is your heart?

God cares about your heart, because all the rest is passing away. If you could somehow live this life forever, the centuries would roll by, and you would watch all your possessions crumble into ruin. Even gold and stone erode. Even as you read this, your body is aging. One day it will die, and you will say good-bye to careers, accolades, retirement accounts, and accomplishments. But your heart—the real you, your decision-making center, the place where your hopes and dreams and desires take shape—your heart will live forever.

CAUGHT YOU DOING SOMETHING *RIGHT*

Many people tend to think of God always watching them, hoping to catch them sinning. They picture a God like Big Brother from Orwell's *1984*, always watching so that they won't step out of line. It's interesting that Jesus didn't have much to say as he watched the rich put in their seemingly large offerings. When the poor widow put in her fraction of a penny, he had something complimentary to say about it. He noticed this tiny offering, demonstrating the way God also notices every last, tiny gesture of goodness we choose to make in this life. No good deed, thought, or act of kindness— no matter how seemingly insignificant in the eyes of the world—escapes the notice of the Almighty. And some of the things that seem small to the world reveal an extravagant and costly faith that matters to God.

One time, as Jesus was reclining to eat with his disciples at the home of a well-respected religious leader, a woman with a shameful reputation came into the room and approached him. She fell at his feet, weeping. She wet his feet with her tears and wiped them clean with her hair. Then she poured perfume on his feet. The religious man thought to himself that Jesus couldn't possibly be a prophet, because if he was, then surely he would know what sort of woman this was who was touching him. Jesus explained that her gesture of kindness actually revealed a heart that had been forgiven. God doesn't look at things the way we do—he sees the heart. The religious leader focused on what was wrong with this woman; Jesus caught her doing something right (see Luke 7:36-50).

It's not that Jesus never condemned or never noticed evil—he was remarkably courageous and outspoken in regard to injustice and sin. That's not the whole picture though. Jesus also noticed good things about people when no one else did. He saw potential where others saw a sordid past. God's heroes need to understand that God sees all the *good* things.

The desire to be noticed isn't always wrong, just often misplaced. God calls us to do things and respond to needs in ways that may never be noticed by people. There are things for which we will never be recognized, and there is a wonderful potential hidden within that reality. There is an opportunity for a secret partnership with God that is much more rewarding than recognition could ever be.

No good deed, thought, or act of kindness—
no matter how seemingly insignificant in the eyes of the world—
escapes the notice of the Almighty.

A SECRET WORTH KEEPING

When Jesus gave instructions about prayer, fasting, and good deeds in Matthew 6, he gave some very countercultural advice along with it. Do your good deeds in secret, he said. For example, when you give to the needy, do so in secret, "then your Father, who sees what is done in secret, will reward you" (Matthew 6:4, *NIV*). Likewise, when you pray, he said you shouldn't make a public show of it, but instead go hide yourself in your room and talk to your Father in secret. "Then your Father, who sees what is done in secret, will reward you" (v. 6, *NIV*). Finally, he said that when you fast, you should take care of your appearance—in today's context, wash your face and brush your teeth—so that it won't be obvious to people that you are fasting, "and your Father, who sees what is done in secret, will reward you" (v. 18, *NIV*).

There's something so intimate about a secret. You would only trust a very close friend with a sensitive secret. When we think about secrets, sometimes we think of "dirty" secrets. We think about things we wouldn't want anyone else to find out about. Here though, Jesus explains that God wants to keep *good* secrets with us. There are things that we actually want other people to know about—we want to be noticed and recognized for them—but Jesus teaches us to keep them as a secret with God.

In Matthew 6, Jesus repeated the same promise three times. Your Father, who sees what is done in secret, will reward you. Jesus didn't explain what the reward is. Perhaps God is more likely to respond to secret prayers or more likely to bless secret acts of righteousness. Perhaps not. Whether any of those things happen, this always does: it strengthens our relationship with God. When we avoid drawing attention to ourselves, our Father who is unseen takes notice.

This is part of the reason why the activity of the church is so hard to measure. Jesus' followers often work behind the scenes.

When you do some act of kindness in secret, knowing that only your Father in Heaven has noticed, you are rewarded with a strengthened sense of his presence. When you pursue God in secret—stealing away for some time at the park, or getting up early so that no one else knows—his friendship slowly becomes more real to you than anything else. And when you begin to understand that God is always watching, and that he notices all the little things you do, it fuels you and inspires you toward the heroic. The secret approval of God is sweeter than any public acknowledgment.

GOD'S SECRET HEROES

This is part of the reason why the activity of the church is so hard to measure. Jesus' followers often work behind the scenes. Sometimes situations call for a public presence or act of service. Sometimes things we do actually make the news. But for every good deed that sees the limelight, there are countless others that are noticed by God alone.

Every once in a while, God allows us a glimpse into the secret activity of his heroes. That happened for my friend Jeremy at his grandfather's funeral. The minister explained how the grandfather had so often beaten them to the punch by helping people in need before the church leaders could get to them. Someone in church would share a prayer request about a lost job or some other financial difficulty. The minister would meet with the elders to consider how they could best come alongside the family and offer assistance. Time and time again, when they visited the family, they found that Jeremy's grandfather had already stopped by to offer some money to hold them over. He always told them the money was "from the church" and not from his own pocket.

Another friend of mine recalled a time when, as a teenager, she found out about her parents' secret generosity. She was convinced that her family could and should move into a nicer house. She even went so far as to do some research and found the perfect house in a much nicer neighborhood and nicer school district. She pestered her father mercilessly about it until he finally sat her down and explained, "Yes, we could afford that house. But we couldn't give near as much money to missions as we do now." In a time when most people were stretching to live above their means, she discovered that her parents intentionally had done the opposite.

I know a man who goes without air conditioning so that he can give more. I don't know how that makes you feel, but I feel like his heart is a step or two closer to God than mine. I'm a total wimp about the heat, and air conditioning is very important to me. I might possibly go without air conditioning to *save* money, but to *give* money? That's what he does. I could name him, but I dare not ruin his wonderful secret.

This relationship with the Lord enables God's heroes to go on serving day after day, year after year, whether anybody notices or not. In chapter 1, we talked about how every ordinary day holds the potential for unexpected adventure—you never know when God will present some unexpected opportunity to do something heroic. Knowing that God is aware of every good deed breathes life even into the days that pass exactly as expected. God is watching, looking at your heart. He wants to share secret conversations and hidden moments. The God of the universe wants to keep private counsel . . . with you.

He doesn't miss a thing. He notices your efforts to serve him or to do the right thing, no matter how seemingly negligible they are to the world. He hears your silent prayers and honors your attention to him. In this life, you will often go unthanked, unrecognized, and unnoticed by others. But you'll find that as you invest in this private relationship with God, he will become more important to you than any of the things you strive to be noticed for in this world. God notices every last thing you do for him in secret that goes unnoticed by others.

The God of the universe wants to keep private counsel . . . with you.

As you develop this humble relationship with him, you will begin to notice his presence everywhere.

RELEASING **YOUR HEROIC** POTENTIAL

1. In what ways is our desire to be recognized natural and good? In what ways is it dangerous or bad?

2. Jesus said that our Father in Heaven would reward us for things done in secret on his behalf. What do you think he meant? In what ways might the Father reward us?

3. What are three practical examples of things you could do in secret for God?

4. Does the fact that God sees everything comfort you, or make you nervous? Or both? Why?

5. If you did some very heroic but unnoticed thing for God, could you keep it secret between you and God for the rest of your life, never telling another soul? If you could, what effect do you think it would have on your relationship with him?

DAILY STEPS TOWARD A HEROIC LIFE

- Think of someone you know who is struggling financially, and plan to anonymously give him or her a gift. Leave the person a gift card for gas or groceries, along with an anonymous note that says, "God provides!"

- Find time to pray secretly. Slip off so that no one knows. Create a "good" secret with your God.

- Direct some money toward something God cares about, in a way that no one else will notice. Use your coffee money, lunch money, allowance, whatever—sacrifice something personal—and give it secretly so that only God sees.

- Practice secret good deeds around the house, at work, at school. Pick up the slack, clean up the mess, fix what's broken, and then never tell a soul. Simply picking up a piece of litter can become an act of holiness when it is done secretly for the Lord.

UNRANKED

ACTS 23:12-24

If you fear God, you need fear nothing else.

 used to be afraid of microwave ovens. I know, that sounds ridiculous. It was. When a microwave was running, I would imagine all the radiation entering my body and causing cancer. I didn't even want to be in the same room when it was on, and would actually avoid it. Even though I knew the fear was unreasonable, I allowed it to rule my behavior.

Go ahead and laugh. I can handle it. At some point, I decided that I was being ridiculous and that I wasn't going to allow an unreasonable fear to rule my behavior. A little to my own surprise, I found that I could make myself stand in the same room with a running microwave with minimal effort. In almost no time, I kicked the fear.

Not so with my fear of sharks. I honestly can't think of anything scarier. This fear is a bit more rational, because let's face it: sometimes sharks eat people. There's nothing irrational about the fear of being eaten by huge predators that lunge from the depths of the ocean at incredible speeds to shred flesh with rows of razor-sharp teeth. The problem is that I allowed that fear to control my behavior.

I have a deep love of the ocean, but for a while I began to avoid going into the water for fear of sharks. It's been said that we're more likely to be struck by lightning than to be attacked by a shark.[1] My fear of sharks was a bit out of proportion with the risk. Fear of lightning never kept me from going out in a storm, but fear of sharks threatened to keep me out of the ocean. Fortunately, my love for the ocean outweighed my fear of sharks.

FEAR MANAGEMENT

I believe that all people have quirky fears that are unique to their personalities or experiences. For you it may be needles, heights, public speaking, or spiders—or all of the above! At their worst, fears have the potential to control us. Other fears are common to everybody's experience, like the fear of rejection, failure, or loss.

So much of life is fear management. Reasons to fear abound. Politicians try to scare votes out of people, painting the picture of doom that only their election could prevent. News media is often fear driven: "Find out what could be killing your baby right now . . . details at 11."

The problem is that I allowed that fear to control my behavior.

Of course, I'm exaggerating. A little. Everyday life does provide a constant stream of reasons to fear though. Some reasons are very serious.

- *They found a lump.*
- *Work is downsizing.*
- *He's never been this late before.*

Fear is not the only, or even the most powerful, motivation—there is love, hope, desire . . . But fear is a powerful motivation. Maybe that's not a bad thing. Marvin Kitman said, "If God wanted us to be brave, why did He give us legs?"[2]

But if there isn't something in us more powerful than fear, or more important to us than the risks, we may never live up to our heroic potential.

On the other hand, living the heroic life that God intended for us requires that we overcome fear. Fear will challenge even the simplest acts of obedience. You may find yourself thinking:

- *If I own up to this mistake at work, I'm afraid the boss will make me the scapegoat.*
- *If I decide to wait for marriage until I meet someone who shares my faith and values, I'm afraid I'll end up alone.*
- *If I forgive that, I'm afraid she'll think she can treat me however she wants.*
- *If I try to build a relationship with that person, I'm afraid he'll just think I'm annoying.*
- *If I help meet that need, I'm afraid there won't be enough left over for me.*
- *If people at school know that I'm a Christian, I'm afraid they'll be watching my every move.*
- *If I commit to serving with the after-school tutoring program, I'm afraid I'll be too busy.*
- *If I tell so-and-so what I really believe, I'm afraid he'll think I'm ignorant and superstitious.*

As we attempt to follow God's lead in this life, we will sometimes face fear. But if there isn't something in us more powerful than fear, or more important to us than the risks, we may never live up to our heroic potential.

Fortunately, there is. Just as my love for the ocean triumphed over my fear of sharks, we can overcome our fears. Our final unnamed hero demonstrated how. In Acts 23, an unranked young man faced great danger from high-ranking enemies, but he didn't give way to fear. We may face different kinds of fears today, but we *can* face them, just the same.

FACING FEAR

The apostle Paul was a powerful, public force for God in the first century—he founded several churches in important cities and spoke the truth compellingly in many places. Paul definitely made a name for himself—even demons knew about him (Acts 19:15). He may not have lived long enough to accomplish some of his greatest deeds, though, were it not for the courage of this unnamed young man.

Paul had recently been arrested and detained by the Romans. The powerful religious leaders were accusing him of heresy, and the Romans were conducting an investigation into the charges. The worst danger to Paul's life, however, was not the Roman courts. The real threat was waiting for him on the road, ready to ambush him and determined to take his life.

No, *determined* isn't the right word. *Deadly serious* is more accurate.

"A group of Jews got together and bound themselves with an oath not to eat or drink until they had killed Paul" (Acts 23:12). These men declared a total fast—no food, no drink—until they had successfully taken Paul's life. Occasionally you'll hear about someone going on a hunger strike until justice is served or some civil rights violation is rectified. You may even hear about some guy who's going to live on the platform of a billboard until his home team wins a game. These men swore off food and drink until they had spilled Paul's blood.

You may have had some enemies in the past. I'm sure there are people out there who don't care for me. But Paul's enemies played in a whole different league. There weren't just one or two of them—or even a dozen. "There were more than forty of them in the conspiracy" (v. 13). *Forty* men swore an oath to God neither to eat nor drink until they had slaughtered Paul.

These forty men went to the elders and the leading priests and said, "We have bound ourselves with an oath to eat nothing until we have killed Paul. So you and the high council should ask the commander to bring Paul back to the council again. Pretend you want to examine his case more fully. We will kill him on the way" (vv. 14, 15). The religious leaders agreed. Not only did Paul have forty incredibly dedicated assassins after him—those assassins also had the blessing and cooperation of the priests and elders. Anyone on Paul's side was up against powerful enemies. Anyone on Paul's side was playing with fire.

Anyone on Paul's side was up against powerful enemies. Anyone on Paul's side was playing with fire.

Somehow, Paul's nephew caught wind of their scheme. I am sure he wanted to do something to help his uncle, but he had some pretty compelling reasons *not* to get involved. This plot had the support of some high-ranking people. Assassins this serious about killing Paul surely wouldn't allow some unranked young man to stand in their way. If the religious leaders were trying to get rid of Paul, there was a good reason to think he had it coming.

But Paul's nephew did not give in to these reasons to fear. Instead, he went to the fortress and warned Paul about the conspiracy. Then Paul called for one of the Roman officers and asked for the young man to be taken to the commander. The officer complied, and the commander took Paul's nephew aside to hear what was so important. "What is it you want to tell me?" the commander asked him (vv. 16-19).

This could have been a frightening moment. Talk about being in over your head! This unranked young man was face-to-face with a commander in the Roman army. Let's not forget that the Roman army not only regularly practiced crucifixion but also had, we might say, perfected the gruesome art.

The young man really stuck his neck out, involving himself in an assassination plot, the scheme of two-faced religious authorities. Even if the commander was neutral in all of this, the religious leaders had money to spend. They could bribe. Men who were willing to swear off food and water would certainly pay the price of Roman assistance in the plot. This young man was unranked and completely at the mercy of these powerful military and religious leaders. He may have been thinking, *What do I want to tell you? I want to tell you that . . . that . . .*

"Some Jews are going to ask you to bring Paul before the high council tomorrow, pretending they want to get some more information." There, he said it. "But don't do it! There are more than forty men hiding along the way ready to ambush him. They have vowed not to eat or drink anything until they have killed him. They are ready now, just waiting for your consent" (vv. 20, 21).

Our unnamed hero's courage paid off.

"Don't let anyone know you told me this," the commander said. Then he called two of his officers and delivered new orders: "Get 200 soldiers ready to leave for Caesarea at nine o'clock tonight. Also take 200 spearmen and 70 mounted troops. Provide horses for Paul to ride, and get him safely to Governor Felix" (vv. 22-24).

This young man was unranked and completely at the mercy of these powerful military and religious leaders.

Imagine the looks on the faces of Paul's enemies as they watched him ride by, mounted high on a Roman horse, surrounded by literally hundreds of soldiers, spearmen, and cavalry. Because of the courage of Paul's nephew, these forty killers became as powerless as one unranked young man. I've always wondered what happened to them. Either they broke their oath and had to live with the shame of it, or died of thirst.

Paul went on to share the good news about Jesus with Governor Felix; and then with the governor's successor, Porcius Festus; and then with King Agrippa; and then finally in Rome with Caesar's own household. Thanks to his nephew's courage, that is.

MISPLACED FEARS

All we know about this young man is that he was the son of Paul's sister and that he took a risk to save Paul's life. Something in his life was more important or more powerful than fear. Perhaps it was loyalty to family, or a desire to do the right thing. Or maybe it was because he feared the *right* thing.

That sounds strange, but Jesus told us not to fear the wrong things. He explained, "Dear friends, don't be afraid of those who want to kill your body; they cannot do any more to you after that. But I'll tell you whom to fear. Fear God, who has the power to kill you and then throw you into hell. Yes, he's the one to fear" (Luke 12:4, 5). That sounds extreme. It is. If you can accept it though, freedom from fear is possible.

Let me explain. We often respond to whatever we fear the most. Consider a situation in which a guy's friends dare him to ask a girl out. How he responds will depend largely on what he fears more: rejection from the girl or the chiding of his friends. When I was a kid, my dad spanked us. Looking back, I'm really grateful for it, because he never punished in anger, and we always knew why we were being disciplined. I never doubted that he loved me, and I respected him. If I had done something really bad, my mom could simply say, "Wait till your father gets home," and I'd immediately regret having smacked my little brother or having lied or having done whatever evil thing had prompted those words from my mother. I had a healthy fear of my dad.

But here's the thing: when my dad was with me, I feared nothing else. I knew that my dad would get between me and anything that would try to hurt me. When my dad was with me, I never worried about being hurt or bullied—or of going without. I had absolutely no doubt that he could and would protect and care for me. So I did fear my dad, but if he was with me, I feared nothing else.

I distinctly remember the time when I lost my breath in the middle of a swim race. I don't know what happened—somehow I pushed way too hard during the first half of the race and my breathing got off timing. Usually a strong competitor, this time I found myself floundering in the middle of the pool, literally gasping for air. I treaded water, sucking as much wind as possible, as the other swimmers pulled so far ahead that placing became hopeless. Then I saw my dad at the end of the pool. He wasn't angry—he looked concerned. And he was encouraging me to slow down and just get to the end of the lap. I did, and he pulled me out of the water. It would have been easy to feel embarrassed or to worry about what my coach would say or to be afraid of whether the other swimmers would make fun of me. Standing off to the side with Dad helping me to slow down my breathing, telling me not to worry, I literally forgot all about the race, my coach, or the ribbons I might have won. There was nothing to fear.

After Jesus explained that we should fear God, and no one but God, he added, "What is the price of five sparrows—two copper coins? Yet God does not forget a single one of them. And the very hairs on your head are all numbered. So don't be afraid; you are more valuable to God than a whole flock of sparrows" (Luke 12:6, 7). He said we should not be afraid—the only one who has any eternal power over you cares more about you than you can imagine. God has compassion on those who fear him, just as a father has compassion on his children (Psalm 103:13).

All too often we fear the wrong things. I wonder if this unranked young man had the courage to delve into this power play between high-ranking religious and military leaders precisely because he feared the right thing. When we have a proper reverence, respect, and fear of the Lord, it frees us from fear of anything else. We don't need to fear humiliation, shame, or even death. Jesus became a man and lived the perfect life and died on our behalf in order to "set free all who have lived their lives as slaves to the fear of dying" (Hebrews 2:15). Simply put, when you fear God, you need fear nothing else.

STRONGER THAN FEAR

Love is so much stronger than fear. Love prompts people to rush into burning buildings, donate kidneys, and to say "I do." I imagine that this unnamed young man's love for his uncle outweighed any fear he may have faced from the authorities. Love—both God's love and love *for* God—is the most powerful force that can prompt the human heart. If you have placed your trust in Christ and committed your life to him, you need not fear, for "as we live in God, our love grows more perfect. So we will not be afraid on the day of judgment, but we can face him with confidence because we live like Jesus here in this world. Such love has no fear, because perfect love expels all fear" (1 John 4:17, 18). This perfect love from God enables everyday people to become heroes in the face of fear.

> This perfect love from God enables everyday people to become heroes in the face of fear.

Sometimes love for God requires the courage to risk our own success and future in this life for something that could last forever. Renate in New York City told me of a young lady who felt very certain about her calling to go and serve as a missionary in Russia. For two years during her studies at a prestigious university, this calling persisted. She simply had to obey. She asked for a leave of absence, but her university refused, explaining that her acceptance would be revoked if she withdrew. Completely unsure of what it might mean for her future, she obeyed God anyway. After completing her two years of service in Russia, she returned to the States and was actually accepted into a better university in a field related to her work overseas.

Two young ladies who are part of my church intentionally moved onto the most dangerous block in the south Bronx in order to live out the words of Jesus regarding the poor. Well-meaning family and friends have discouraged them and said things to make them afraid. But they have persevered to develop loving relationships with their neighbors: drug dealers and gangsters, but also single moms who've adopted other people's kids and are doing the very best anyone could with what they have. A relationship with the Father brings supernatural courage in the face of reasons to fear.

One close friend of mine spent last year working in the inner city of Philadelphia, where he met a number of courageous unnamed heroes and learned a bit about following God in spite of fears. He recently wrote a letter to people who'd been praying for him throughout that year.

He explained that he and some of his housemates had been going with a local pastor to minister to heroin addicts at a warehouse in the inner city. The only other people who ever went there were the heroin addicts, and his descriptions of the place conjured up images of a real hell on earth. On this particular occasion, the pastor was called away. Something prompted my friend and two female housemates to go in for the first time without the pastor's guidance.

Here's what he said:

We walked. The first man passed and I said nothing. I could see he was just trying to get out, to go use, and be on his way. We walked. We talked with someone; then the dealer saw us and started to tell us to get out. This was by now a routine, but for the first time, someone threw a few glass bottles about ten feet in front of us.

We walked. We talked to two gentlemen, who after talking to us, could not shoot up in front of us, so they went to another room. We ran into the dealer again and had a rather long conversation. We prayed for him, but he walked away somewhat angered. I followed him. We kept walking. Some men entered with baseball bats.

My friend said that, for whatever reason, he didn't think much about that. One of the ladies with him spoke to these men in Spanish for a bit, and then they prayed with them.

My friend said, "Later I saw one of them exiting with a gun." My friend did not have a sense of peace; he was actually very scared. But something compelled him to keep walking. "I would not describe it as an obedience to the love of God," he wrote. "I'm not that obedient. The only thing I know is that I am a broken lost person, and he came and gave me a home, gave me a name."

Next, my friend did something strange. "There were a few cement bricks in the warehouse. Often, people would put their needles on them while they got other stuff ready. They were altars—places where people gave their lives away. Following the example of King Josiah [2 Chronicles 34], I destroyed one of the blocks, one of these 'Asherah poles.'" Instead of crushing it, though, he "destroyed" its power by turning it into something good. He picked it up and took it home. "Now I pray over it," he wrote. "It is being redeemed, it is now an altar to God, a place I go to give my life to the True King."

He "destroyed" its power by turning it into something good.

Little did he know then that something incredible would happen.

The next day, the warehouse was shut down for renovations. "It hasn't been touched in years," my friend said. "I have to admit, I didn't believe it until I saw it, totally clean, nothing on the ground, no one inside."

FACING GOD

Living for God often requires courage. Sometimes we have to be bold in what we say, even when we know we're out of our league. Sometimes we have to confront somebody or stand up for what's right. Sometimes our integrity requires us to take a stand that can jeopardize our jobs or social standing. Sometimes we have to defend the powerless or unpopular. And taking any step of faith—to serve, to love, to communicate about Jesus—requires courage. But if we have a proper, healthy fear of the Lord, we can be unafraid.

Whenever you feel any unrest, anxiety, or fear—whenever anything threatens the peace in your heart—the thing to do is to focus on God. Don't ever attempt to conquer fear through some force of will. If you try to face fear this way, you'll find yourself like Peter, who, after defying the forces of nature and actually walking on water toward Jesus, turned his attention for a moment to the wind and the waves, and began to sink (Matthew 14:30). If you focus on yourself or the fear you face, it only will make things worse. But if you keep your eyes on Jesus, you can face anything. Being unranked in the world does not mean you don't rank with God. He defends the weak, gives wisdom to those who ask for it, and gives power to the powerless.

Dorothy Bernard said, "Courage is fear that has said its prayers."[3] Always invite God into your fears. He knows precisely how you feel—he knows it even better than you do. Don't ever hide from him. Hide *in* him, but don't hide *from* him. In the same way that we open our uncleanness to him and our uncertainty to him, open your fears to him. Whenever you fear, focus on Jesus.

Even if you are the last person anyone would expect God to use; regardless of how unclean you are; although you are completely unpolished; no matter how unworthy you are; even if you're totally underestimated, unnoticed, and unranked—you can be unafraid. Keep your eyes on him.

I don't know what opportunities you may have in this life to do something heroic. I don't know when you'll be called on to act courageously. I don't know what good works God has "prepared in advance" for you to do (Ephesians 2:10, *NIV*). Whether it's to stand up, speak up, or own up—whether it's to risk your life or your livelihood—I know that you will need courage to follow Jesus.

You can be one of God's unnamed heroes—if you'll live with courage.

Be strong and take heart. Remember always that God is with you. Fear him only, and you have nothing to fear. Love him with everything you've got, and his perfect love will conquer your fears.

RELEASING **YOUR HEROIC** POTENTIAL

FOR INDIVIDUAL OR GROUP STUDY

1. What are you afraid of? Spiders? Public speaking? Needles? Heights? Why?

2. Have you ever responded to a dare? What happened? Were you afraid? What was the outcome?

3. How do you react to the concept of "the fear of the Lord"? In what ways should we fear him? In what ways shouldn't we?

4. Which do you think is more common, physical courage or moral courage? Why? Which is more difficult? What makes it so? Which is more important? Why?

5. Has there ever been a time when you failed to act out of fear that you didn't "rank" high enough to be heard? How about a time when you acted in spite of having to stand against someone of higher rank?

6. Is there anything that you would like to do for God that requires courage? What is it? What frightens you about it? What do you think it would take for you to overcome those fears?

DAILY STEPS TOWARD A HEROIC LIFE

- Take some time to journal about your fears. What are you afraid of? Very honestly list anything that you currently fear. Then invite God into those fears. Affirm his power and your love for him—then ask him for courage.

- Practice focusing on Jesus. Whenever you experience unrest, fear, or anxiety, return your focus to him. Don't focus on the problem; focus on Christ's power, presence, and love for you.

- Fear the Lord. Get your relationship in right orientation with Jesus. If you are anything less than 100 percent surrendered, identify the points at which you are still holding back, and let go. Submit to him. Give his perfect love complete access.

- Read Psalm 27. Pray it. Memorize it so that when you are tempted to fear, you can meditate on its words.

NAMED

— REVELATION 3:5 —

God's people have an everlasting name.

wish we had space for some of the others—for Pharaoh's daughter, for the woman who washed Jesus' feet with her tears, for other stories of modern-day unnamed heroes. As you've read these stories along with me, I hope that you've looked at your life and your God through the lens of Scripture and seen things as they really are.

A GLIMPSE OF REALITY

Real things last forever. God "has planted eternity in the human heart, but even so, people cannot see the whole scope of God's work from beginning to end" (Ecclesiastes 3:11). But we can get a glimpse of it through the lens of the Bible. There, in the ancient pages of Scripture, we get to see some of what happens *after*. Jesus said, "All who are victorious will be clothed in white. I will never erase their names from the Book of Life, but I will announce before my Father and his angels that they are mine" (Revelation 3:5).

Jesus said he would *never* erase the names of those who belong to him. Whatever name your parents gave you will fall out of knowledge, just as your birth certificate will disintegrate, your body will decompose, and your achievements will fall to ruin. The Bible only records the tales of very few of God's heroes, and even some of them are unnamed. But the Bible isn't the only record of the exploits of his people. Every last follower of God is recorded in the Book of Life.

We are all *named*.

A NEW NAME

Sometimes we fear that following Christ will mean losing our identity. It does not. Look at how wonderfully unique each one of God's followers in the Bible is. I would argue that the longer we follow God and the more like Jesus we become, paradoxically, the more unique we become. Our individual gifts, passions, and purposes are more fully realized and energized.

Jesus said he would *never* erase the names of those who belong to him.

A few of my students help me do things around my classroom, like taking down bulletin boards or filing student work—and I look for little ways to repay them. Earlier in the year, I made a drawing of one girl's name, with the letters colorfully done to simulate a rainbow. Then I gave it to her as a way of saying thanks.

Wow, it was a hit! All my students wanted one. Then other students saw them and wanted one. Then students I don't even teach wanted one. I've now produced a dozen or so of these drawings, and I'm deeply backordered. Free sells fast.

The art is mediocre. You can definitely get something much nicer from the airbrush artists in Times Square. But then, many of my students have

never been to Times Square (or more than twenty blocks from their housing project, for that matter).

I close my eyes and try to envision the essence of who each young person
is, and then try to capture it in the drawing.

One little guy who's so full of juice you could power the lights off him
got his name drawn with bright flames curling up around the letters. One
young lady's name was rendered in a drawing of purple glass, because there
is something elegant and graceful about her spirit. A young man who is as
tall as I am and a bit bigger (truly a giant of a man in the making), but who
is gentle and quick to smile, received his name made out of sections of red
brick wall. I told him, "Because that's how I see you. Just solid. Trustworthy. Loyal."

When it came time to draw Sara's name, I wasn't sure how to do it. She's
a behavioral nightmare. She makes it very difficult for anyone to like her.
When I calmed myself and considered how to make a drawing of her name,
the unlikely word that came to mind was . . . *precious.* I made the letters of
her name out of different-colored gemstones, each sparkling. On the back
I wrote, "Because Sara is precious."

There is a verse from Revelation that has haunted me ever since I first
read it. It has left a kind of sweet aftertaste in my heart that has changed the
flavor of everything since. Here's what it says: "I will also give him a white
stone with a new name written on it, known only to him who receives it"
(Revelation 2:17, *NIV*).

A new name given by Jesus. A name known only to me . . . to Sara . . . to
you. A name so utterly unique, so unmistakably individual, so you-and-no-
other that it can only be known as a secret. Surrendering your life to Christ
actually means setting foot on a path toward *finding* your true identity. It
means hearing from the One who knows who you really are, the One who
knows your name.

When Simon correctly identified Jesus as the Messiah, Jesus gave him
a new name: "Peter (which means 'rock')" (Matthew 16:18). Jesus named

him The Rock. Never mind that Peter would later chicken out and deny Christ. Jesus saw his ultimate end, saw beyond the cowardice, beyond the denial, saw the man who tradition tells us asked to be crucified upside down because he didn't consider himself worthy to die in the same position that his Lord had. Jesus gave him the name of what he would become.

It's not easy for me to see Sara as precious. Obnoxious, nasty, difficult, cruel . . . but precious? I have to close my eyes and calm down to see it, but I think I'm seeing the truth about her.

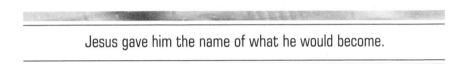

Jesus gave him the name of what he would become.

Am I more loving than God? He knows what a funny notion that is. My love and God's love—apples and oranges, my friends. Apples and *galaxies*.

In God's perfect love, he can clearly see what he wants us all to become. He sees what he wants *me* to become. And I want to become that. So what name will he give me? Oh, I can dream. I can hope. But I'll bet it will be better than anything I come up with.

What name will he give you?

NOTES

CHAPTER 1

1. Story from Michael Garofalo, "A Victim Treats His Mugger Right," NPR's *Morning Edition,* March 28, 2008, http://www.npr.org/templates/story/story.php?storyId=89164759 (accessed July 1, 2009).

2. Tom Brokaw, quoted in *Reader's Digest,* September 2001, no other information available.

3. "For Want of a Nail," quoted from http://www.gather.com/viewArticle.action?articleId=281474976762779.

CHAPTER 2

1. Mickey Mantle, http://www.bellaonline.com/articles/art31788.asp (accessed 6/30/09).

CHAPTER 3

1. John Wooden, www.wisdomquotes.com (accessed 6/30/09).

2. Mark Twain, www.thinkexist.com.

CHAPTER 4

1. According to Michael J. Wilkins, "Entering the home of a Gentile rendered a Jew ceremonially unclean (cf. Acts 10:28)." *The NIV Application Commentary: Matthew* (Grand Rapids, MI: Zondervan, 2004), 342.

2. Oren Harari, *The Leadership Secrets of Colin Powell* (New York: McGraw Hill, 2002), 42.

CHAPTER 5

1. John Henry Newman, www.brainyquote.com (accessed 6/27/09).

2. Edgar Watson Howe, www.brainyquote.com (accessed 6/27/09).

CHAPTER 7

1. From "The Calzone," *Seinfeld,* written by Alec Berg and Jeff Schaffer, originally broadcast April 25, 1996, http://www.seinfeldscripts.com/TheCalzone.htm (accessed 8/12/09).

2. Austan Goolsbee, "Now That a Penny Isn't Worth Much, It's Time to Make It Worth 5 Cents," *New York Times,* February 1, 2007, http://www.nytimes.com/2007/02/01/business/01scenes.html (accessed 8/12/09).

CHAPTER 8

1. Jennifer Copley, "How to Reduce the Risk of Shark Attacks," Suite 101, http://fishinsects.suite101.com/article.cfm/how_to_reduce_the_risk_of_shark_attacks (accessed 9/13/09).

2. Marvin Kitman, www.quotegarden.com (accessed 6/30/09).

3. Dorothy Bernard, www.quotegarden.com (accessed 6/30/09).